Practical Observations on the Lord's Prayer

by C. Matthew McMahon

Copyright Information

Practical Observations on the Lord's Prayer, by C. Matthew McMahon, Ph.D., Th.D.
Edited by Therese B. McMahon

Published by Puritan Publications
A Ministry of A Puritan's Mind in Crossville, TN
www.apuritansmind.com
www.puritanpublications.com
www.reformedsynod.com
www.gracechapeltn.com

First Electronic Edition, 2026
First Modern Print Edition, 2026
Manufactured in the United States of America

eISBN: 978-1-62663-538-8
ISBN: 978-1-62663-539-5

Table of Contents

Introduction 4

Chapter 1: Sensible Prayer 13

Chapter 2: Hallowing God's Name 40

Chapter 3: Thy Kingdom Come 64

Chapter 4: Thy Will Be Done 85

Chapter 5: Daily Bread 104

Chapter 6: Forgive Us Our Debts 122

Chapter 7: Lead Us Not into Temptation 149

Chapter 8: Deliver Us from the Evil One 170

Chapter 9: Thine is the Kingdom 200

Chapter 10: Conclusion 230

Other Works by Dr. McMahon at Puritan Publications 235

Introduction

Okay, so here's the deal with this book—it's not just another dusty theology tome, and I'm not just saying that. I've been wrestling with prayer my whole life, and I mean *wrestling*. You know how it goes: you're on your knees, or in a church service, muttering the Lord's Prayer like it's some magic spell, half-expecting God to just nod and hand you what you want. But then you *read* Matthew 6:9-13, and Jesus is like, "Pray *this* way," and it hits you—there's something deeper here. That's what *Practical Observations on the Lord's Prayer* is about. It's nine sermons I poured my heart into, explaining what Jesus meant, and it changes the way a person should speak with God.

This book takes every bit of that prayer—every line, from "Our Father" to that final "Amen"—and cracks it open, like a walnut. Each chapter digs into one part, not just to explain it (though there's plenty of that, with all the Reformed theology and Puritan grit you'd expect), but to make it hit home. Like, what does it mean to call God "Father"? It's not just a word—it's a gut-punch reminder that we're His children, not some random nobodies begging for scraps. Or "Hallowed be thy name"—that's not just saying God's holy; it's a call to live like His holiness matters *more than anything*. And don't get me started on "Thy kingdom come" or "Deliver us from evil"—those aren't *throwaway lines*. They're about longing for God's rule to break into this broken world and fighting the devil's schemes with every ounce of faith we've got.

I'll be honest, preaching and writing this was not easy. I kept thinking, "Who am I to unpack *Jesus'* prayer?" But the more I dug, the more I saw how this prayer isn't just words—it's a map for living. It's about praying with *sense*, not just rattling off wants or chanting like some papist with a rosary. It's about letting God's Word shape your heart, making you want what He wants, not the other way around. Sometimes I'd finish a sermon and feel like I'd barely scratched the surface, but then I'd pray it myself, and it was like God was saying, "Keep going, you're getting it."

Look, if your prayer life feels stale—sometimes wondering if God's even listening—this book's for you. It's not *fancy*, but it's raw and real, pulling from Scripture and ministers like Manton, Luther, Perkins, *etc.*, who knew how to pray like their lives depended on it. It'll push you to rethink what you're asking for, why you're asking, and whether you're ready to let God remake you through it. It's a guide, sure, but it's also a challenge: stop babbling, start praying sensibly, and watch how it changes *everything*. You'll see God's glory in a new light—His kingdom, His power, all of it. And that "Amen" at the end? It's not just the finish line; it's your heart saying, "Yes, God, I'm in."

This book, *Practical Observations on the Lord's Prayer*, born from nine sermons that God in His mercy pressed upon my heart, is no mere academic treatise. No, it is a personal confession, a heartfelt guide, drawn straight from the forge of my own trials and triumphs in prayer. I write not as some lofty theologian perched upon an ivory spire, but as a brother in the fray, one who has groaned under the weight of unanswered cries and rejoiced in the sweet assurance of a Father's embrace. If you, like I once was, find your prayers echoing hollow in the chambers of heaven—vain repetitions, as our Savior called them, heathenish babblings that presume to twist the Almighty's arm with our multitude of words—then take heart. For herein lies the remedy: *sensible prayer*. Not the rote recitation of a rosary or the frantic listing of wants, but a prayer that draws from the deep well of Scripture, conforms our rebellious wills to God's eternal decrees, and ascends as sweet incense, transforming us even as it honors Him.

Consider, friend, the scene in Matthew 6, where Christ, seated upon that Galilean hillside, turns His eyes upon His disciples—those rough-hewn fishermen and tax collectors, no doubt fidgeting with the same restless hearts we bear today. "After this manner therefore pray ye," He says, and oh, what a manner it is! Not a formula to be mindlessly parroted, but a blueprint for the soul's communion with the Divine. "Our Father which art in heaven"—words that pierce me still, evoking the tender ache of a child orphaned by sin, yet adopted into the family of the King. How often have I whispered these in the dead of night, feeling the vast chasm between my frailty and His holiness, yet drawn nearer by the Spirit's gentle tug? This preface alone revolutionizes our approach: no longer do we storm the throne as strangers or debtors alone, but as beloved sons and daughters, confident in His fatherly care, yet humbled by His heavenly majesty.

As we journey through this prayer *clause by clause*—hallowing His name, yearning for His kingdom's coming, submitting to His will as in heaven so on earth, beseeching our daily bread, pleading forgiveness as we forgive, crying for deliverance from temptation and evil, and sealing it all with the doxology of His eternal kingdom, power, and glory—we uncover not just doctrines, but *living truths* that have reshaped my own devotions (and they will do that for you).

Praying sensibly, as this book unfolds, means just that: prayer with sense, with understanding, with the mind illumined by the Word. It is no accident that Christ prefaces this model with warnings against the hypocrites' showy displays and the heathens' empty chatter.

Why pray at all, if God knows our needs before we ask? Because, my friend, prayer is not to inform the Omniscient or persuade the Immutable; it is to mold us, to align our crooked desires with His straight path. In my early days, I treated prayer as a divine negotiation, bargaining for blessings as if God were a reluctant merchant. But oh, the liberation in discovering that true supplication echoes the Psalms—the very *songbook* of sensible praise—reminding the Father of His own promises, not to jog His memory, but to steady our faith. "Thy kingdom come"—how this petition has fueled my intercessions for the church, for lost souls in my congregation, urging me to labor not for earthly empires, but for the Spirit's greater sway in hearts and homes.

Yet, as we delve deeper, we must confront a grievous shadow that looms over our modern age, particularly in the Evangelical church of our day. Here, I pause to offer a candid critique, for the Spirit compels me to speak plainly, as one who loves her yet weeps over her follies. Alas, what has become of prayer in the Evangelical fold? Once a mighty engine of *revival*, a furnace where souls were refined and heaven invaded earth, it now languishes as a shallow puddle, lapped at by the thirsty but quenching no true thirst. How many pulpits thunder with calls to "just pray about it," yet leave the flock adrift in a sea of ignorance, mistaking recitation of wants for communion with the Divine? They gather in mega-sanctuaries, lights flashing like a *carnival*, bands crooning emotional anthems that stir the flesh but *not* the spirit, and when the altar call comes, what do they pray? A hasty litany of needs— Lord, bless my job, heal my aches, give me that promotion"—as if the King of kings were a cosmic butler summoned to fetch and carry. Vain repetitions, indeed! Christ warned against such heathenish babble, yet here it thrives, unchecked by any sense of God's sovereignty or the soul's depravity.

Oh, the tragedy! Evangelicals should be seeing themselves as heirs to the Reformer's and Puritans' legacy, and yet, now treat the Lord's Prayer as an optional addendum, a quaint relic trotted out at weddings or funerals, stripped of its doctrinal sinews. They recite it mechanically, if at all, supposing that "good intentions" suffice, as if faith without knowledge could ever please the Omniscient One. William Perkins rightly decried such ignorance centuries ago: "Very few among the people can give the right meaning of the words of this prayer... ignorant men are to learn the right meaning." Yet today, in coffee-shop Bible studies and podcast devotionals, prayer is reduced to positive affirmations, a self-help *mantra* where God is petitioned not to hallow His name first, but to rubber-stamp *our* agendas. Where is the awe before "Our Father in heaven"? The submission to "Thy will be done"? Instead, it's "My will be done, amen!"—a subtle idolatry that crowns man as sovereign and God as servant.

This kind of prayer which theological illiteracy breeds in a church anemic in power, rife with superficial conversions that wither under trial, is really deplorable. They cry for "daily bread" as material excess, blind to its call for trust amid want; they mouth "forgive us our debts" without the bitter pill of forgiving enemies; they beg deliverance from evil while courting it through worldly alliances. No wonder scandals rock their leaders, their families are train wrecks, and revival tarries! For sensible prayer demands self-examination, a wrestling with sin's chains, a conformity to Scripture that exposes our hypocrisy. Evangelicals, wake from this slumber! Cease your babbling auctions at heaven's gate; learn the pattern Christ gave, or your prayers rise no higher than the ceiling, an abomination to the Holy One. Repent, and pray aright— for His glory, not your gain.

Returning now to our path, dear reader, let this not discourage but spur you onward. In the chapters ahead, we shall unpack each petition with practical fervor, showing how "Give us this day our daily bread" teaches contentment in providence, freeing us from the anxiety that gnaws at modern hearts.

And what of "Lead us not into temptation, but deliver us from evil"? In my battles with the world, the flesh, and the devil—those ancient foes that prowl like shadows in the soul—this plea has been my shield. Temptation comes not as a thunderclap, but a whisper, suited to our weaknesses by a cunning adversary. Yet God, faithful Promiser, tempers it to our strength, turning even falls into sanctified lessons if we but cry out. I have stumbled, oh yes—into pride's snare, lust's thicket—but each deliverance has deepened my reliance on the Spirit, who intercedes with groanings too deep for words.

Finally, the doxology: "For thine is the kingdom, and the power, and the glory, forever. Amen." Here prayer crests into praise, a thunderous ascription that reminds us that all petitions orbit His glory. In my quietest moments, this has been my anchor: not my eloquence, but His sovereignty assures the hearing. Amen—so be it! A testimony of faith, sealing our desires in Christ's merits.

Also consider the cover. It is a little "celestial," but the Lord's Prayer is celestial. It is like a doorway that opens us to God's work. It is our prayers aligning with His decree. So that doorway into heaven—that idea—is captured in the cover: that passageway into a more celestial life, which is exactly what the Lord's Prayer opens up for us. Jesus is teaching us to pray. Jesus is showing us how to align our wills with His sovereign Kingship. It is as though the doors of heaven swing wide open when we settle ourselves into that pattern and outline of prayer. Consider it.

As you turn these pages, let them be a companion in your closet prayers. Practice them, not as drudgery, but delight; let the Spirit quicken these truths in your heart. For *sensible prayer* is the Christian's breath, the pulse of eternal life beating against the world's clamor. May God, our Father, draw you nearer through these words, that your supplications might avail much, your life hallow His name, and your soul rest in His unshakeable kingdom. To Him be glory everlasting. *Amen.*

In Christ's grace and mercy,
C. Matthew McMahon, Ph.D., Th.D.
From My study, February, 2026
"...search the Scriptures..." (John 5:39).
www.apuritansmind.com
www.puritanpublications.com
www.gracechapeltn.com
www.reformedsynod.com

Chapter 1: Sensible Prayer

Matthew 6:5-13, "And when thou prayest, thou shalt not be as the hypocrites are: for they love to pray standing in the synagogues and in the corners of the streets, that they may be seen of men. Verily I say unto you, They have their reward. But thou, when thou prayest, enter into thy closet, and when thou hast shut thy door, pray to thy Father which is in secret; and thy Father which seeth in secret shall reward thee openly. But when ye pray, use not vain repetitions, as the heathen do: for they think that they shall be heard for their much speaking. Be not ye therefore like unto them: for your Father knoweth what things ye have need of, before ye ask him. After this manner therefore pray ye: Our Father which art in heaven, Hallowed be thy name. Thy kingdom come. Thy will be done in earth, as it is in heaven. Give us this day our daily bread. And forgive us our debts, as we forgive our debtors. And lead us not into temptation, but deliver us from evil: For thine is the kingdom, and the power, and the glory, for ever. Amen."

Jesus, amid the weighty teachings of the Sermon on the Mount, instructs his disciples on the sacred art of prayer. This sermon is directed squarely to those followers who gathered around him as he sat to expound upon the truths of the Old Testament, serving as a kind of ordination address. For if one is to be a faithful disciple, commissioned to venture forth into the world on behalf of the Messiah to proclaim the Gospel, certain foundational principles must be etched upon the mind—one of these being the proper manner of communing with God, drawing from His own word.

In this passage, Christ imparts essential, commonplace truths about prayer, such as the reality that God rejects certain prayers offered wrongly and insensibly. There are boasting prayers, performed ostentatiously in public, which garner reward solely from the admiration of men—as the hypocrites do. Likewise, there are babbling prayers, in which men suppose they shall be heard for their multitude of words. Rosaries exemplify such vain repetitions; so too does the rote prescription of reciting twenty Our Fathers and ten Hail Marys, or kneeling thrice daily to intone a fixed formula. *Do not imitate them*, Jesus admonishes, for such practices are devilish.

Instead, Christ delineates the fitting time, place, and manner of prayer: "But thou, when thou prayest, enter into thy closet, and when thou hast shut thy door, pray to thy Father which is in secret; and thy Father which seeth in secret shall reward thee openly." In solitude, in intimate communion, at the appointed hour—such secret closet prayer draws divine reward. Indeed, good works performed sensibly yield heavenly recompense.

It is undeniably true, as Christ affirms, that God knows the needs of His people before they utter a word. This truth provokes a pressing inquiry: if God possesses omniscience, discerning every necessity prior to petition, why pray at all? Is this not a reasonable question? Moreover, if God is immutable—unchanging, with decrees ordained before the world's foundation—what alteration does prayer effect? Does it sway God's will or mind? Nothing alters God, ever; He remains eternally *immutable.*

Why, then, pray? God commands it, and that suffices. Yet, to probe further is to uncover a fundamental practical truth: if prayer changes neither God's mind nor His eternal plans—if it is not a means to coax or compel Him—what *purpose* does it serve? Many have imagined that through eloquent, fervent, or forceful entreaties, God *might be persuaded* to align His will with theirs, crafting arguments so convincing as to bend the divine purpose. But prayer exists to transform *the one who prays.* It conforms the supplicant's words to what God has already declared, decreed, and revealed in His Scripture.

One might counter: is not prayer simply a catalog of desires and needs? Not in such crude simplicity. Submission to God's will demands a continual struggle against human frailty, for men possess no power to alter even a single hair upon their heads. They present petitions to God because He cares for them—they know this assuredly—yet they must yield their wills to His, aligning righteous prayers with His decrees, or rather, shaping prayers to mirror those decrees. This, in turn, compels the question: what has God decreed? What has He spoken?

Prayers that ascend as sweet incense into heaven's throne room arise from the heart, offered in privacy where God alone hears, according to His will and in the Spirit. In this way, Christ enumerates nine facets of prayer—the manner in which it must be conducted, to accord with God's will. If they are absent, it ceases to be prayer. Understand this: without these, *it is no prayer*. What Christ prescribes is a pattern for praying, not a mechanical rosary. In essence, distill the Psalms—the *songbook* of divine praise—into a framework of supplication, and one approximates what Christ has established. God's word is reshaped into an argument and returned heavenward, reminding Him—from the one praying—of His own promises. Does God forget His utterances? Or does He desire His *people* to grasp them fully, praying sensibly to harmonize their wills with His? This truth revolutionizes how Christians ought to conceive of prayer.

So, Jesus delineates these elements: "Our Father in heaven," evoking filial thoughts, as of a family bond. "Hallowed be thy name," petitioning for holiness and the reverence due to God, both in word and deed. "Thy kingdom come," yearning for the fulfillment and consummation of all the Messiah inaugurates in God's realm, with eager anticipation of the Spirit's greater sway in daily life. "Thy will be done in earth, as it is in heaven," the quintessence of submission to God's sovereign law. "Give us this day our daily bread," beseeching provision for life's necessities, free from fret or fear. "And forgive us our debts, as we forgive our debtors," confessing sin while extending compassion to others. "And lead us not into temptation, but deliver us from evil," utter reliance upon God against the assaults of darkness, wickedness, the world, the devil, and the flesh. "For thine is the kingdom, and the power, and the glory, for ever. Amen," concluding in doxology, acknowledging His eternal sovereign rule manifest in His kingdom.

Doctrine: Sensible prayer directs God's people to draw near to the Father with humility, delight and confidence, according to his word.

Briefly considered, prayer stands as that Christian duty performed toward God by sensible and believing souls. The term "sensible" is pressed here in a dual sense—mindful attention to its usage is warranted. What rule has God furnished for directing his people in prayer? The entirety of God's Word serves to guide them therein, yet the paramount rule emerges in that form of prayer which Christ imparted to his disciples, commonly termed the Lord's Prayer.

To contemplate it properly begins at the preface. What does the *preface* of the Lord's Prayer convey? "Our Father which art in heaven" instructs God's people to approach Him with holy reverence and confidence, akin to children before a father both able and eager to aid them, and further, that they should pray alongside and on behalf of others.

In this vein, prayer, as divinely commanded, constitutes a duty—a facet of the worship owed to Him by his people. Scripture abounds with both patterns and precepts concerning it: "So Abraham prayed unto God," (Gen. 20:17). "And he withdrew himself into the wilderness, and prayed," (Luke 5:16). "After this manner therefore pray ye," (Matt. 6:9). Christians require divine assistance, and their most pressing needs find supply solely in Him who is All-sufficient. When his people approach God in prayer, it manifests their belief in His power and mercy to succor them in every exigency, and signals their readiness to receive the aid He has ordained—provision for necessities, comfort, and relief alike.

The sensibleness and fervency of prayer furnish compelling evidence of one's salvation—a thorny predicament for many who profess belief, is it not? As Nathaniel Vincent observed, "The child, when born, cries; and the sinner, when born again, prays."[1] For the apostle Paul, upon his conversion, it was noted, "behold he prayeth," (Acts 9:11).

Prayer must be directed to God alone: "Thou shalt worship the Lord thy God, and him only shalt thou serve," (Matthew 4:10). "I will direct my prayer unto Thee, and will look up," (Psalm 5:3). What need exists to petition another? A saint in heaven? An angel? Are they more *capable* than Christ? None but God can fulfill the Christian's every need, "according to his riches in glory by Christ Jesus," (Phil. 4:19).

The word "sensible" applies to prayer in two respects. First, it pertains to the experiential manner of prayer—whether one's devotions prove rote, arid, and mechanical, or vibrant, stirring, and potent. Only true Christians grapple with such distinctions; the wicked remain indifferent to repetition or ritual, content so long as some vague sentiment of accomplishment lingers. Professing Christians might well heed this caution: mere feeling avails nothing.

Second, sensibleness demands praying rightly. A correct mode of prayer exists, alongside erroneous ones; the latter, devoid of true essence, devolves into something else entirely—a truth many professing believers resist, convinced that their every effort suffices. Prayer severed from God's Word constitutes the wrong

---

[1] Nathaniel Vincent, The Spirit of Prayer, eBook, (Puritan Publications 2012).

path. Conversely, prayer anchored in Scripture aligns with righteousness, demanding wisdom and discernment attuned to God's will. Those who pray must embody sensibleness in both senses. Jesus did not license haphazard supplication but prescribed a scriptural manner. Nowhere does God declare, "Pray as you please." Ignorance, unbelief, and hardness of heart render words a mockery before God if uttered amiss and absent the Spirit—hence the wicked cannot truly pray, their efforts deemed an abomination. In this way, effective prayer requires sensibleness in manifold aspects: wisdom and illumination to pray aright. If effectual, fervent prayers avail much, then ineffectual, languid ones achieve naught.

This necessitates *knowledge*—awareness of sins and needs amid a fallen world. All Adam's progeny stand in dire want. They must acknowledge their unworthiness for any petition to be heard or heeded; God owes them no obligation. As Job confessed in 40:4, "Behold I am vile, and I abhor myself." What claim could fallen Adam's children assert to merit divine favor? Yet, they recognize that none except God, through Christ by the Spirit's power, can aid them. What other advocate or intermediary suffices but Christ, via the Spirit, to the Father?

It follows that those who pray must be believing souls, grounded in the Word's truth. Faith is indispensable to all duties; only the redeemed can bring

Jesus Christ into every act. This does not absolve the fallen from duty's obligation, yet it remains incumbent. Absent faith, God receives no honor from duties, nor do performers profit thereby. "If the Word be not mixed with faith, it will not profit us," (Hebrews 4:2); likewise, prayer devoid of faith and Scripture yields no benefit, regardless of verbosity. Such supplications prove ineffectual. Effectual fervent prayers exist, alongside those that falter—some prevail, others avail nothing. Those who pray must be believers, exercising duties in faith.

They must believe "that God is, and that he is a rewarder of them that diligently seek him," (Hebrews 11:6)—harboring right conceptions of His gracious nature and benevolence toward men. He wills reconciliation, peace through Christ, abundant life in Him, and walking in the Spirit per Scripture's precept and pattern. He dispatches ministers to instruct His people therein, that they might know His identity, character, and will as revealed in His Word—enabling supplication in every form, aligned therewith. Absent this, prayer falters. Even Christ's disciples, long in His company, implored, "Lord teach us to pray"—a plea, in its Greek nuance, beseeching guidance on manner, words, and form. Or, rendered plainly: how shall one converse with God to ensure hearing, answering, and sensible assurance?

Those who pray aright must be invested in the Word's truth concerning the Mediator and Savior, Jesus Christ. If "no man cometh unto the Father but by him," (John 14:6), then prayer *sans* Christ proves impossible. If prayer in the Holy Spirit (as Jude enjoins) is requisite, then the Trinity entire engages in rightful prayer: to the Father, in Christ's name, by the Spirit's power—yet how? *According to the Word.* Absent this, one babbles in self-devised fashion. Christ, received by faith *per* the Gospel He proclaimed, unites believers to Him as spouse; they entreat accordingly, by His words. He denies naught beneficial or needful, per Scripture. All in such filial union find God as their God and Father, akin to Christ Himself, loved as He is loved (John 20:17 and 17:23).

Such believers lean upon biblical promises—abundant in the Old Testament, fulfilled in the New. In this way, to pray well, demands acquaintance with both. Upon what did the disciples rely when Christ taught prayer? By faith, they "rely on the promises that God has made." Moments after delineating prayer, did He not declare, "they that ask shall receive, that they which seek shall find, and to them that knock it shall be opened," (Matthew 7:7)? How else but by rightful petition?

As prayer recurs daily—"give us this day our daily bread"—so does confidence multiply when God fulfills promises. They correlate His scriptural assurances with providential outworkings, attuned to

His ways. Therefore James exhorts asking "in faith, not wavering," (James 1:6), and Hebrews urges drawing near "in full assurance of faith," (Hebrews 10:22). Belief, wedded to prayer, aids overwhelmingly: Christians pray Scripture *as they believe it*. "Therefore I say unto you, whatever things ye desire when ye pray, believe that ye receive them and ye shall have them," (Mark 11:24). It entails hearty conviction that God, per His covenant for Christ's sake, pardons sin and grants sufficiency in requests aligned with His Word—truths discerned as His will. Herein, promises materialize in real time.

Thus, all petitions accord with His will, as children submit to a father. Not according to what they imagine God's will to be, or merely hope it might be, but according to what it truly is. One might inquire, what is God's will for my life? They ponder and wonder at God's purposes. But *why* the uncertainty? What compels such speculation—*what would Jesus do*? It is inscribed by the Spirit in the Word. To pray well, they must turn there, wielding it as a sword—the Spirit's sword—for battle, for fervent and effective supplication. His will resides in it; one might protest, I seek God's will for my personal life, and that does not lie in the Word. Oh, but it most *certainly does*, for all things pertaining to life and godliness are therein contained.

That is why the Bible repeatedly declares the Word to embody God's will—His will of precept—and exhorts Christians to pray in accord with it. If they prove lazy and ignorant of it, how then shall they pray? Will they be heeded for their multiplicity of words? Will they prevail by *arguing God* into conformity with their notions? Prayer, approached biblically, undergoes a radical transformation for the informed Christian.

In the *preface* of the Lord's Prayer, Christ teaches his disciples to draw near to God with confidence—how so, confidence? Such instruction gathers from His portrayal of divine all-sufficiency as Father, and His readiness to aid them. Not only is God prepared to help, but He does so with filial affection; as a Father, and they ought to regard Him as such—is this not precisely the terminology Christ employs? In response, since He first loved them, they stand ready to submit to Him with desire, love, and delight, even as children to a father.

The title Christ bestows upon God for His people's address is "our Father." This constitutes, the manner in which Christians petition the Almighty. This form or pattern of prayer positions the Christian in the solitude of the closet for private devotion, performed in secret, yet directs them to employ a plural style in their addresses. They do not enter alone and declare, "My Father," but in that secret communion, they pray to "our Father." "Have we not all one father? hath not one God created us?" (Malachi 2:10). Such usage implies that Christians must acknowledge the vast scope of the Godhead in His universal power and goodness toward all His people—His 144,000, His perfect covenanted church. They are not to arrogate God vainly and proudly to themselves *alone*. They possess brothers and sisters within this grand Kingdom of God, covenant members sharing equally in it. In this way, in their devotions, they ought to remain exceedingly mindful of those mutual bonds knitting them as people and Christians in God's family—manifold relations forged in covenant, redemption through Jesus Christ, and the enlivening power of the Holy Spirit, who quickens and reminds them of their spiritual union. They should harbor hearty goodwill and charitable affection toward one another, not seeking merely their own private good, but that of all brethren as they petition "Our Father." Christ did not bid them say "my Father," but "our Father who art in heaven," teaching their common paternity and enjoining brotherly goodwill even in solitary prayer. When alone, they are not truly alone; *others* demand consideration and thought.

The designation "our Father" orients the Christian mind to their relation with God. God is their Father (1 Chron. 22:9–10; Isa. 63:16; Matt. 6:9; Matt. 23:9; John 20:17; Rom. 8:15; Gal. 4:6; Eph. 3:14–15; Heb. 12:9). They are adopted by God through Christ, with Christ as their brother in this regard (John 20:17; Rom. 8:29; Heb. 2:11–12). The Father is "our Father" inasmuch as: He granted them being, fashioning them in His image by creation; and He preserves and sustains them continually by grace—that is, by redeeming them from the law's curse, whereby the image He bestowed is renewed daily in righteousness and holiness.

This description, "Father," among all God's names, titles, and attributes, proves most fitting for the duty of prayer, spurring them to approach in a manner that heightens their sensibility as His children and as partakers in a communion greater than themselves. In this way, Christ instructs His people not merely to regard God as God—which they assuredly must—but as *Father*, to request life's provisions as a father would for his children. He can and will, *per* His declared promises, supply their needs according to His will, in His way, and in His time, as their Father. What do they need? How does one discern the answer to that query—what do they need? They need whatsoever the Word of God declares, and therefore the Father shall provide all such necessities. They must look there to furnish context for every petition or need they voice. Such awareness will engender thankfulness to the Father, manifesting filial respect and affection toward Him. Is it not innate for children to flee to their parents in need or peril? That title, "Father," urges them to run to Him for everything.

What comprises all things they require? Again, they must consult the Word for illumination. Moreover, it reveals not only His power and authority over them as Father, but His affection and tender regard. They will engage this effectively and sensibly by drawing near in all things according to His Word. This, then, illustrates the *posture* Christians ought to adopt toward God: approaching not solely with profound reverence and exalted thoughts, but with humble affection and sincere gratitude for His fatherly provisions in every necessity. By invoking God as Father, they express love for Him, declare fidelity, repose hope in Him, and believe in His benevolent disposition to aid them for the sake of what He has wrought in His Son.

God is the believer's Father by the mediation of Christ, and certain consequences attend drawing near to God the Father in prayer. By faith, they are united as one with Christ, and in that oneness, God becomes their Father. This affords wonderful comfort to the Christian who *knows* God as his Father. In John 20:17, as Christ prepared to depart from His disciples, He instructed Mary: "Go tell my brethren, that I ascend to my Father and to your Father, to my God and your God." In Gal. 4:6, "He hath sent the Spirit of his Son into your hearts, whereby ye cry, Abba, Father." This constitutes a great comfort and blessing—that they may boldly, yet reverently, address God as Father with "Abba, Father," the *utmost respect* tendered to Him, all secured through Jesus Christ.

Seeing God as their Father, they strive to please, respect, and obey Him in every course and action, as children should or ought. And as Christ Himself declared, as exemplar, that He came not to do His own will but the will of His heavenly Father, so believers must affirm: "Lord, I have not come to do my own will, but to do the will of my heavenly Father." They delight in such obedience. For if He is "our Father," they will eagerly comply with all His commands, provided they ascertain them. Where shall they discover those joyful imperatives to perform according to His directives?

Seeing God as their Father, they labor to resemble Him as closely as possible; for a child yearns to emulate his father, and if men profess to be God's children, they will endeavor to mirror Him in all holiness and righteousness. Eph. 5:1 commands, "Be ye therefore followers of God as dear children." They resemble Him in the holiness of life. As 1 Peter 1:17 warns, "If ye call him Father, which without respect of persons judgeth according to every man's works, pass the time of your dwelling here in fear; and be ye holy, for he is holy." It is evident how the wicked ape the ways of their forebears, or like their father the devil: Jer. 44:17 recounts, "Even as our fathers have done before us, so will we do." Wicked folk eagerly trail their progenitors, drawing nigh in imitation. How much more, then, should believers hasten to follow the paths of "our heavenly Father"?

Seeing God is "our Father," His people must trust and rely upon Him as a Father, drawing near to Him to entrust their cares in this life to His keeping. The Father knows His children require all "these things," and therefore they come in prayer, beseeching His fatherly care for every need. They observe how God has tended His people in times past, according to His Word, a truth that greatly aids their sensibleness in prayer—for as the Father has helped His children before, so He will again. Will not God, out of His fatherly care, provide for them through the good means He has appointed, as He has promised? Does not His Word declare it so? And herein lies the crux: where *in the Word* is this found? What comfort can Christians glean if not from the Word itself? They draw near in prayer to rely wholly upon Him, trusting because of what He has spoken and accomplished. As the Psalmist attests in Psalm 23, God in His fatherly care will prepare a table before them, supplying all their needs. If God is "our Father," He will provide for them.

Moreover, seeing God is "our Father," chastisements sometimes befall His children, and they ought to receive such from the hand of a loving Father. They are to bear them patiently. The Psalmist declares in 39:9, "I was dumb and said nothing, because it was thy doing." David affirms in 1 Sam. 3:18, "It is the Lord, let him do what seemeth him good." And what did Christ Himself pray to the Father in Luke 22:2, "Father, if thou wilt take away this cup from me; nevertheless not my will, but thy will be done." Every affliction serves as a messenger from the Father, and believers should accept such from His hand as that which works for their good. They ought to bear it patiently, an integral facet of drawing near to the Father as they should. They must be content to relinquish anything or undertake any task the Father requires, discerning this through careful attention to His Word.

They draw near to Him as Father in humility, submitting to His will; in delight, knowing He cares for them; and with confidence, assured through Christ who secures their filial standing. All these form compelling arguments to approach God sensibly as Father with prayers that prove effectual for His glory and their good.

God is Our Father. Such is a simple application for believers. Seeing that God is our Father, we ought never to be disheartened in our prayers to him. We have not yet anatomized those prayers in any depth, but for the present, let us hold fast to this: God is our Father, and he loves to hear his children pray to him. If a child falls sick, how does a father yearn to help? How ready, do you think, would such a father be—with all tenderness and care—to extend his hand in aid of his son or daughter? What if that child grew gravely ill, teetering on the brink of death, growing ever weaker until words failed, leaving only a gaze fixed upon the father's face, eyes brimming with tears, moans escaping in sighs and groans that bespoke mounting pain and unspoken longing? What would such expressions do to a father's heart? Would they not pierce him deeply? Would he not swell with profound compassion, eager to succor his child? And what, then, of our heavenly

Father? When we draw near sensibly in prayer, our strength ebbing until we can but lift our eyes to him, moaning and groaning in wordless plea, will he not show tenderness and compassion, lifting us by his power and mercy? He will, for he is our Father. In fact, "Likewise the Spirit also helpeth our infirmities: for we know not what we should pray for as we ought: but the Spirit itself maketh intercession for us with groanings which cannot be uttered," (Rom. 8:26). Through the Spirit—our Interpreter—the Father discerns those groanings and sighs, bearing such ascending prayers, moaned and groaned and yearned for, up to heaven's throne.

We ought not to grow discouraged in drawing near to God as Father if our theological eloquence falls short of our desires, or if we cannot pray with the fluency of others. Scripture transforms this for every believer: by taking God's words and forging them into arguments, how can we err? Sanctification unfolds as a gradual schooling, degree by degree. Step by step, we traverse the path of holiness; day by day, we besiege heaven's throne with boldness, emerging refined in prayer. There is striving, and in that striving, betterment. Yet the Father is captivated by even *one* of our glances, by a single chain about our necks (as the Song of Songs 4:9 attests), for Christ Jesus accompanies us in prayer. We draw near under his mantle, and all is accepted by the Father *through him*—we ourselves are accepted. We cannot always pray as we wish; we stammer, stutter, falter in articulation, imperfect in our discourse, often fumbling to shape God's word into a cogent plea. But the more we learn, the more we voice truths aligned with his will and decrees; the more we know, the more sensible we become to what the Father delights to hear from his children. Our heavenly Father takes pleasure in the broken utterances of his children's prayers, offered with upright hearts as lively, hearty, and orderly sacrifices per his word. They ascend as sweet incense, enveloped in Christ's blood—for the Father beholds his Son arising before him, and these are the saints' prayers according to the Word, praying the Word, with Christ as the Word incarnate. This excuses no laxity in sensibleness or growth in prayer, yet it imparts confidence to approach boldly: even in prayer's direst straits, the Spirit aids with unutterable groans and sighs—not as pretext, but as the capstone of effectual, fervent prayers that avail much.

When we behold a father cradling his infant in his arms, we deem the child secure in such proximity to one who holds him fast. The babe clutches his father's fingers, tiny hands gripping with all the feeble strength little arms afford—but where comes the true strength, if not from the father's embrace, not the child's grasp? So it is when we draw near to God: we clasp his hand, as it were, with our prayers' frailty and faltering vigor, falling short of our ideals; yet the strength resides in the Father who upholds us. By faith, through Christ's power and the Spirit's might, we bind ourselves to him in prayer.

Oftentimes, our infant-like faith seems to loosen its hold (or so it appears to us), our grip on him weakening, our sense of him dimming. There we cry out, beseeching his aid, striving to reclaim that awareness—for we crave the union of knowledge and experience. What we know as truth, we yearn to feel sensibly in prayer. Behold how this conception reshapes the entire domain of supplication! Though we may sense his distance, we still desire to rest in his arms like an infant; he holds us steadfast—do we grasp this?

Yet *you* are often disappointed in yourself, failing to draw near as desired, losing that sense more than gaining it. Consider a father tasking his daughter with some laborious chore; she applies her utmost skill and strength, yet her effort pales beside what he might achieve. Upon completion, she beholds her shortcomings and weeps over them. What earthly father, witnessing such tender-heartedness, would not melt with paternal affection, overlooking every flaw despite her earnest striving to please? And shall God our Father extend less mercy and pardon to his children, who willingly heed his call to draw near in prayer, sorrowing heartily that they cannot do better? No, surely—he accepts their labors because Christ accompanies them. This bolsters no excuses for childish endeavors, but reveals the Father's compassion toward his offspring; and yet, children grow. A prayer may be clumsily framed upon some truth, uttered in rudimentary degree or rote fashion—perhaps rehearsed before—yet God will affix it to his celestial fridge, even if scrawled with broken crayons of sorts. For his Spirit conveys those prayers heavenward, interpreting them so that the Father receives them in Jesus Christ, crayon or no; he displays them for heaven's hosts, knowing they spring from his child's heart.

It is common for Christians to lament God's seeming distance, a waning sensibility of his presence in prayer. If God is our Father, we should not succumb to discouragement if his nearness feels vivid one moment and veiled the next—if he seems to hide his face even as we labor earnestly in prayer. Sometimes the sun conceals itself behind clouds for a spell, and we savor its warmth all the more come tomorrow. At times, our lives linger under prolonged overcast. The sun does not withdraw itself; certain *sensations* merely obstruct its rays. Clouds intervene, and Christians must discern them sensibly. Oftentimes, sin stirs such hindrance, demanding our attention. "Why art thou cast down, O my soul? and why art thou disquieted in me? hope thou in God: for I shall yet praise him for the help of his countenance," (Psa. 42:5). God our heavenly Father tends us with infinite tenderness, upholding and preserving us in every circumstance, even when his proximity eludes our senses.

There is great comfort in drawing near to God as Father in prayer this way. Seeing God as our Father, we are summoned to a dignity and honor surpassing any worldly accolade. What greater elevation exists than to be called God's *sons*? As 1 John 3:1 exclaims, "Behold, what manner of love the Father hath bestowed upon us, that we should be called the sons of God." Seeing God as our Father, he will remain so eternally through Christ: "And will be a Father unto you, and ye shall be my sons and daughters, saith the Lord Almighty," (2 Cor. 6:18). He fulfills a Father's duties. No earthly parent could do more for his child than God does for us; none, in any era or place, stands readier to aid than our Father. Psalm 103:13 attests, "As a Father hath compassion on his children, so hath the Lord compassion on them that fear him." And since God is our Father, he bestows a heavenly inheritance through Christ Jesus—unfading, eternal in the heavens, as promised. The Father grants this realm, as Christ assures in Luke 12:23, "Fear not little flock, for it is your Father's will to give you a kingdom." Heb. 11:16 declares, "wherefore God is not ashamed to be called their God: for he hath prepared for them a city." He provides not merely earthly sustenance through prayer, but an eternal, heavenly patrimony for his people; there, all find fulfillment, prayers cease, perfection reigns. Is this not partly why we pray "thy kingdom come"? Assuredly more encompasses it, yet this forms a portion. An eye toward consummation, all perfected—and intriguingly, such a daily entreaty.

Here in prayer unfolds a beholding of God, by the bond of Father to children. Approach him with the encouragements at hand; cast yourselves upon him, drawing near in supplication. If you are a believer, he is your Father by creation and by redemption alike. Yield not to weakness or faintness; fix not on this sin or that, but go to him, call him Father, plead his word on your behalf. Entreat with lowliness and modesty, great love and singular delight in him, bold in holy assurance of God's love in Christ, as gospel-promised. Prayer fosters all this—and such resides merely in the Lord's Prayer's preface, God as our Father.

The Father commands prayer in Scripture. Numerous passages enjoin it: the Lord bids us "pray always," (Luke 21:36,) "to pray everywhere," (1 Timothy 2:8) "to continue instant in prayer," (Romans 12:12) "in everything by prayer and supplication, to make our requests known unto God," (Philippians 4:6)—for he wills to bestow necessities, conveying mercy without which misery prevails. Prayer draws us near, knitting us closely to him. And he promises much therein: "The effectual fervent prayer of a righteous man availeth much," (James 5:16). Not merely the *prayer*, but the effectual, fervent prayer of such avails much—many professors delude themselves, deeming closed eyes and uttered words suffice duty. Does Scripture furnish patterns? By prayer, Abraham obtained a son when Sarah was barren. By prayer, Jacob escaped Esau's wrath. Jonah emerged from the fish's belly. Shadrach, Meshach, and Abednego survived the sevenfold-heated furnace. David halted the plague when it gripped Jerusalem, sheathing the angel's sword. Elijah sealed the heavens for three years and six months, then unlocked them to fructify earth. Joshua stilled the sun over Gibeon. Daniel muzzled lions, exiting unscathed. Peter, Paul, and Silas burst from prisons, shackles, iron cells—frail barriers to prayer's power and God's will. Such righteous, valiant prayers prove effectual when wielded aright. This should spur us to love and practice this duty fervently.

Prayer's utility offers grand encouragement, especially as Jesus delineates its pattern. Employed through Christ to the Father, in the Spirit's power, your prayers delight God. "...the prayer of the upright, is his delight," (Proverbs 15:8). "O my dove, that are in the clefts of the rock, in the secret place of the stairs, let me see thy countenance, let me hear thy voice, for sweet is thy voice, and thy countenance is comely," (Song of Solomon 2:14). We delight in our children's prattle, be it lisping infant babble or whatever their age permits. God indulges infinitely more than earthly parents; far readier to bestow good (Matthew 7:11). He fixed his love upon us before the world's foundation. We are his Son's blood-bought treasure, ransomed at life's cost for sin's remission. Covenanted with God, he pledges to be ours—assuredly our Father. Vessels of mercy, destined for eternal glorification of his grace and love. In this way, he heeds when you pray; grants needed good, shields from besetting evil. Herein find humility, delight, and confidence in drawing near.

Such prayer, rooted merely in this initial facet—God as *our Father*—might resemble this:

> I come to bring glory to you, O Lord, who in teaching me to call you Our Father, have taught me not to confine my love to myself, but to pray also with brotherly affections for all mankind, especially the household of faith. I see children of earth by creation, and Christians by adoption, all under one heavenly Father. O grant me brotherly kindness to them, that I plead identical blessings for them as myself, earnestly praying they share your Fatherly love. In teaching us to pray to Our Father in Heaven, you reveal the infinite chasm between God and us—to supplicate with a beggar's humility, a creature's awe, a sinner's tremor before Creator and Judge. O Father, you fill all places, yet your glory blazes in heaven, where your majesty dwells resplendent; there we lift hearts in prayer. Let my soul soar to you in heavenly thoughts, desires, love. Savor no earthly taint when I approach, as you are in heaven! You

teach seeking heaven foremost; you, Father, first. Grant, Lord, that I plead blessings in due order—with holy violence, persistence, resolution, as love's essencc, vital to eternal welfare.

Consider Question 100 of the catechism. *What doth the preface of the Lord's Prayer teach us? Answer: The preface of the Lord's Prayer, which is, Our Father which art in heaven, teacheth us to draw near to God with all holy reverence and confidence, as children to a father, able and ready to help us; and that we should pray with and for others.*

In the next chapter we will consider the first petition of the Lord's Prayer as it pertains to *holiness*.

Chapter 2: Hallowing God's Name

Matthew 6:9, "After this manner therefore pray ye: Our Father which art in heaven, Hallowed be thy name."

The initial segment of the Lord's Prayer concerns the preface, or invocation, addressed to our Father—an address that invokes God as the collective head of the church body, to which the Christian stands organically and covenantally bound.

The subsequent portion of the Lord's Prayer unfolds through *petitions*. The preface's opening, invoking God as Father, bears an adjunct: that He *resides in heaven*. This reminds Christians of *their* proper station in submitting to the Father enthroned above. He is not merely in heaven, but reigns there in a peculiar sovereignty, governing all from that exalted seat. God dwells and rules in heaven. As in Luke 15:21, "Father, I have sinned against heaven, and against thee." Or Luke 20:4, "Was it from heaven, or of men?" It portrays God as King—a truth Christians should have contemplated often, and therefore I'll not belabor His celestial kingship, except to affirm its reality: "The LORD hath prepared his throne in the heavens; and his kingdom ruleth over all," (Psa. 103:19). With that established...

The inaugural petition encapsulates the aims and design of the ensuing petitions, the prayer's conclusion, and even the Decalogue, within whose framework this prayer resides comprehensively. One who has not traversed the Ten Commandments, nor pondered them deeply, shall *scarcely grasp the Lord's Prayer*; the two are *inextricably* interwoven.[2]

This first formal petition directs itself to the reigning Father in heaven, beseeching that He be held holy in a singular fashion: "Hallowed be thy name." It petitions for holiness and the honor due to holiness, to be rendered and manifested toward the Father. The plea fastens particularly upon God's name. Through this name, Jesus gestures toward all that constitutes Theology Proper—the doctrine of God Himself—encompassing His titles, attributes, ordinances, Word, and works, by which He deigns to reveal Himself. When God is denominated Almighty, it evokes a *holy potency* unveiled. When merciful, a holiness infuses His clemency. When just, His justice operates in unalloyed sanctity across all affairs. His providence unfolds in holiness, His Word breathes holiness, His works proclaim it—for His essence is holiness, and even His names are hallowed.

---

[2] See my work, *The Ten Commandments in the Life of the Christian.*

One must then inquire: does God improve through prayers that His name be rendered more holy? Can such a thing be?

The manner in which Jesus frames this petition may strike as *peculiar*. Is not the Father already holy—indeed, the quintessence of holiness, the primordial and preeminent Being in this regard? Does not God's effulgence, His radiant essence, embody holiness unalloyed? Verily, God is holy in His nature; yet the petition presupposes that His name is not invoked holily in every sphere surrounding it, as befits His majesty. This entreaty forms a vital thread of worship, dictating how worship ought to express itself in the Christian's life—for the Christian's existence, in its entirety and every facet, orbits around holiness.

Doctrine: The Father is to be regarded as holy in His titles, attributes, ordinances, Word, and works.

To hallow God's name is to sanctify it, to set it apart as holy in all things. "Hallowed be thy name" means nothing less than "Let thy Name be made holy in all things." The contemporary church stands in grave peril here, for many are not captivated by holiness. They content themselves with offering God whatever suits their fancy, presuming it suffices. Yet is the luster of God's holiness—the eminent glory of His being—truly preferred above all else in their lives? Is their zeal wholly fixed upon that which is holy?

The first petition of the Lord's Prayer centers on exalting God's glory above all and dedicating this service as utterly holy. It echoes, in part, the initial commandments of the Decalogue. The first commandment instructs Christians to walk holily with their God, to have no other gods before Him, and to embrace Him as He reveals Himself in holiness through His Word—a weighty demand, requiring deep knowledge of its meaning. The second commandment prohibits worshipping God amiss, enjoining worship in holiness as prescribed by His Word. The third commandment forbids using anything pertaining to God—His name, titles, attributes, ordinances, Word, or works—outside the realm of holiness, insisting they be regarded as separate and sacred. God's glory reigns supreme, the chief end of all creation and the ultimate purpose of His counsels. As Prov. 16:4 declares, "The Lord hath made all things for himself; yea, even the wicked for the day of evil." Thus, whether eating, drinking, or undertaking any act, Christians do all to God's glory, upholding His commandments to honor His titles, attributes, ordinances, Word, and works as holy. The chief end of man revolves around God's resplendent glory, manifesting His power in the world. The highest aim of any Christian endeavor—or any human endeavor—is to glorify the living God, to be captivated by the Father's radiant luster, desiring His titles, attributes, ordinances, Word, and works be glorified by men.

William Perkins aptly noted the ignorance surrounding this prayer: "Very few among the people can give the right meaning of the words of this prayer. They pretend, that seeing God knows their good meaning, it is sufficient for them to say the words and to mean well. But faith being one of the grounds of prayer, and there being no faith without knowledge, neither can there be prayer without knowledge, and therefore, ignorant men are to learn the right meaning of the words."[3] God's name in this petition encompasses His titles, attributes, ordinances, Word, and works—all that pertains to God Himself and His actions, including attributes like holiness, justice, mercy, and truth, His providential works, and His judgments. His Word reveals His character and will comprehensively; Scripture brims with His names, and all attached there falls under this petition. Why not say "hallowed in all His words" or "works"? Why confine it to His name? Because naming God's glory equates to naming His holiness—His attributes, titles, and works. As Abram "builded an altar unto the LORD, and called upon the name of the LORD," (Gen. 12:8), Christ, in this petition, instructs His disciples, as dear children, to hallow God's

---

[3] William Perkins, *An Exposition of the Lords Prayer in the Way of Catechisme* (Edinburgh: Robert Walde-graue, printer to the Kings Maiestie, 1593), 24

name, *separating* it from vain things. To hallow is to set apart from common use for a sacred purpose, as the tabernacle, temple, or ephod were uncommon, or as the Lord's Supper transcends daily meals, and the Lord's Day elevates the common week. Such are consecrated to God's service, deemed holy.

What, then, shall Christians do but hallow God in His titles, attributes, ordinances, Word, and works? The third commandment forbids using God's name—or anything related—in vain, reinforcing that His titles, attributes, ordinances, Word, and works must be treated as holy. The commandments and the prayer's petitions intertwine fundamentally; to misunderstand the law's role is to misapprehend right prayer, for they complement and build upon one another. All believers in Christ are set apart as holy, sanctified for a sacred purpose, united to the holy, harmless, undefiled Savior. In honoring His name, they fulfill their baptismal covenant, upholding God's titles, attributes, ordinances, Word, and works. In this lies the Christian life's sum: doing His will (the commandments) and praying for His will to be done (the petitions). Their lives become living sacrifices to His holy nature and will. Do they pray daily that God's name be hallowed? Is it their foremost petition, as it was Christ's first to the Father?

How can a sinful, albeit redeemed, person hallow what is already perfectly holy, as the Father is? God is unassailably holy in His titles, attributes, ordinances,

Word, and works: "For thy Maker is thine husband; the LORD of hosts is his name; and thy Redeemer the Holy One of Israel; The God of the whole earth shall he be called," (Isa. 54:5). Annexed there is the exhortation, "Follow peace with all men, and holiness, without which no man shall see the Lord," (Heb. 12:14). God's name, pure and holy, cannot be made holier. Why, then, this petition? Christians pray not to augment God's holiness but to declare and manifest it through their lives and works, rightly employing His name. What will the contemporary church answer on judgment day, entrusted with stewarding holiness—to hallow God's name and proclaim it holy to the world—yet distracted by lesser pursuits? Christians must manage the right use of His name, ensuring it remains pure, honorable, and holy, radiating a zeal that burns as a shining light, a city on a hill for weary travelers. Curiously, this petition does not primarily aim at global conversion, nor does the Lord's Prayer contain an explicit missionary plea—a striking pause for reflection. Yet, this first petition, alongside the concluding call for the Kingdom's coming, declares God's character to the world, subtly embedded in missions. Christians become beacons of holiness, prompting inquiries from those around them about the hope within. Their eminent holiness should spur the unsaved to ask what makes them distinct. Therefore, Christians zealously strive to be consumed by God's holiness, walking to maximize the glory of His holy name. But how, if they do not know God in His holy titles, attributes, ordinances, Word, and works?

This petition, though concerning the Christian, centrally regards God and the believer together. It is no digression but a *linchpin*, encapsulating the *Christian life* in *holiness*. Praying for the sanctification of God's name as separate and holy, Christians pray for themselves, seeking to stand as children before the Father, ever pursuing holiness. Christ places this petition first, urging believers to prioritize the Father's holiness above personal or communal needs under "Our Father." They must crave holiness foremost, a pursuit impossible without understanding God's perfections or their own fallen nature. In this way, Christians first seek holiness for themselves and others.

What is *holiness*? It denotes the moral perfection of God's nature in its excellence and beauty—His divine, uncreated essence, wholly separate and undefiled. God cherishes all that is holy and detests all that opposes Him: "Once have I sworn by my holiness that I will not lie unto David," (Psa. 89:35), swearing by Himself, the epitome of holiness. Holiness also resides in what saints gain through salvation, enabling them to emulate the Father as dear children, striving for purity, partially freed from sin's defilement, longing to mirror God's holy and pure nature. As Hebrews 12:14 declares, "Without holiness no man can see God." Believers live, move, and exist in holiness, which encompasses all duties directly tied to God and His worship—their entire life. Ephesians 4:24 speaks of "holiness and righteousness of truth," pairing holiness with uprightness against wickedness. This petition to hallow God's name in service and demonstration forms part of the fall's reversal, addressing sin both indirectly and directly.

God's *holiness* is twofold: communicable and incommunicable. In its communicable aspect, born-again Christians partake of holiness through the Spirit's transformative work (reformation), receiving a new heart to reflect God's holiness in inward thoughts and outward deeds. This reflection manifests in three spheres: the holy law of God; the Spirit's work in transforming believers into new creatures, a work of holiness; and the duties of those set apart for worshipful service to the Father. In its incommunicable aspect, none is holy as God is holy. His holiness, intrinsic to Himself, cannot be fully imparted to any other: God is morally perfect, incapable of evil, resolved to every morally excellent act per His law and character. As 1 Samuel 2:2 proclaims, "There is none holy as the Lord," and the psalmist in 99:9 exhorts, "Exalt the Lord our God, and worship at his holy hill; for the Lord our God is holy." Even God's name is holy: "Holy and reverend is his name," (Psa. 111:9), the crux of this petition, strengthening the Christian's resolve to uphold the commandments, particularly to not take the Lord's name in vain. God is intrinsically holy, separate from all that the fall introduced into creation's goodness—utterly perfect, free from evil, at liberty to exercise His will flawlessly. He never transgresses His law, nor lacks conformity to it, for He cannot deny Himself; what He is as holy, He always does. So profound is His holiness that the seraphim encircling His throne cry ceaselessly, "Holy, Holy, Holy is the Lord God Almighty," (in Isaiah 6), veiling their eyes before Christ's radiant glory, praising in submission to His kingship—a delight resounding in God's ears. This forms the substance of the first petition Christians utter daily.

In believers, holiness is a quality fashioned in the heart by the Holy Spirit, cleansing and purifying them for pure worship of God: "Blessed are the pure in heart: for they shall see God," (Matt. 5:8). Purity of heart equates to holiness, signifying both living before God now and, ultimately, beholding His perfections' luster in heaven. When believers assemble, they form a holy temple, fitted as holy bricks by the Spirit's work in union with Christ—the beauty of holiness: "...worship the LORD in the beauty of holiness," (Psa. 29:2). In the Old Testament, holiness was engraved upon the band on Aaron's forehead and chest (Exod. 28:36-38), marking the high priest—a type of Christ—and all pertaining to him as consecrated to God. Zechariah 14:20-21 alludes to this: "In that day shall there be upon the bells of the horses, HOLINESS UNTO THE LORD; and the pots in the LORD'S house shall be like the bowls before the altar. Yea, every pot in Jerusalem and in Judah shall be holiness unto the LORD of hosts: and all they that sacrifice shall come and take of them, and seethe therein: and in that day there shall be no more the Canaanite in the house of the LORD of hosts." This signifies that believers' actions and possessions are consecrated to God, even their *pots*. Revelation 14:1 echoes this: "And I looked, and, lo, a Lamb stood on the mount Sion, and with him an hundred forty and four thousand, having his Father's name written in their foreheads." The hallowed nature of God's name is the first petition—holiness to the Lord. The term "holiness" is ascribed to God, His throne in heaven (Psa. 47:8), Mount Zion (Psalm 48), His Spirit (Rom. 1:4), and to man as a duty to hallow His name (2 Cor. 7:3; 1 Thess. 1:13), regarding Him in a distinct light.

Scripture delineates four kinds of holiness: unlimited in God's infinite holiness; limited in Christ's human nature, perfect yet human, distinct from His unlimited divine nature; supported and unlimited in the holy Scriptures, dependent on God yet demonstrating all facets of His holy nature and will; and for men and angels, reliant on God's Spirit and limited by their nature. Anything that reverses the fall's evil or attains good per God's nature is commended in this petition. Believers, reliant on Christ for holiness, are limited by indwelling sin and their finite nature, necessitating prayer that God make them holier, acting in accord with His holy name.

This petition for holiness raises the distinction between the covenant of works and the covenant of grace. How could it not, when contemplating holiness? It recalls the law's demand to love God with all heart, soul, mind, and strength—a standard unmet except through honoring Him above all. Christians cannot pray rightly unless they prioritize the sanctification of His name, the highest calling in life, to be regarded as holy by themselves and others. Glorifying God's name, often through praise in Scripture, here entails a prayer and its outworking—separation from sin and worldliness unto sanctity, itself a form of praise. One cannot pray this petition intelligibly without familiarity with God's titles, attributes, ordinances, Word, and works to praise Him. Christians grow in holiness by degree, praying daily to reflect on holy things tied to God's nature. The more they learn, the more they understand, drawing nearer to the Father through the Son in the Spirit's power, aware of their limited holiness, relying on the Spirit and Word. God's holy name must occupy center stage in every Christian's thoughts each time they pray.

Did not Christ commence with the holy name of Father, *collectively*, in the invocation? His name, holy in itself—"Our heavenly Father," an otherworldly Father intruding into time and space with a message of reversing sin and the fall—demands hallowing.

Christians prove their belief by praying and living in holiness that matches His name. God desires His people to hallow His name, glorifying it to reflect their reverence for Him, both to Him and to themselves.

The name of God must be considered in two respects: as Christ describes Him, "Father," or through names reflecting His character—Almighty, All-Seeing, and the like. A name distinguishes one person from another; how much more do God's perfectly holy names distinguish the manifold facets of His perfections? To glorify His name, as His Word prescribes, demands familiarity with His titles, attributes, ordinances, Word, and works—else one cannot pray this petition intelligibly. God's names are unique to Him, shared by none, for holiness is His character and essence. Yet His name is to be magnified as such. Christians must ever seek deeper knowledge of God in His titles, attributes, ordinances, Word, and works (Lev. 24:11), pursuing all means to know Him, especially His Word and works (Psa. 8:2; 1 Tim. 6:1). His titles, works, Son, worship, holy words in law and gospel, creation, providence, salvation, and redemption are recorded in Scripture. In these, God gloriously displays His power, wisdom, loving-kindness, truth, mercy, justice, and righteousness. As Godefridus Udemans exhorts, "We should thus proclaim and praise these works in all sincerity."[4]

---

[4] Godefridus Udemans, The Practice of Faith, Hope, and Love, ed. Joel R. Beeke, trans. Annemie Godbehere, Classics of Reformed

Under God's name lies a duty to use all associated things—His titles, attributes, ordinances, Word, and works—in a holy manner. Places and things deemed God's are to be consecrated to holy use, most notably His people. Every place where God sets the remembrance of His name, where His government and providence in redemption operate, where He blesses His people through Christ Jesus, is regarded as holy. There, where believers unite organically to Christ in His death and resurrection, God's holiness descends like rain, distilling within them to draw them nearer to the Father. The Spirit, through Christ, blesses the assembled people for His worship—the place of preaching, praise, sacraments, and all means of grace, where His name's impression marks their foreheads and manifests in their lives. In all these, God's name is imprinted, and Christians, praying this petition, contemplate its vast scope. Through these, they regard His name as holy, holding it in high estimation, loving such lofty thoughts because their sanctification arises when God magnifies Himself in and through them.

Christians primarily pray to account all things associated with God's name *as holy*, making His name great and glorious among men through their declaration, their lives, and their very prayers. When they esteem all

---

Spirituality (Grand Rapids, MI: Reformation Heritage Books, 2012), 126–127.

things tied to His name as holy, they glorify God, desiring that His name be highly regarded as holy and used holily in all things. In exercising knowledge of His titles, attributes, ordinances, Word, and works, they maintain a holy regard for the loftiness of His name. Lancelot Andrewes observed, "The name Aaron had as High Priest on his headband was not glory, but holiness to the Lord, (Exod. 28), and the four beasts ceased not to cry day and night, Holy, holy, holy, Lord God Almighty," (Rev. 4:8).[5]

Christians who dwell on such holy things, by experience, know that God's holy name often lacks the reverence due, both in themselves and others. Failing to uphold His holiness in His titles, attributes, ordinances, Word, and works, they recognize His name is taken in vain. They know, as with Elimelech or David, that such sin often incurs God's plagues and vengeance. Do Christians pray against the contemptuous abuse of God's name as central to their daily supplications, or do most *scarcely* consider it, more preoccupied with trivialities like a broken weed-whacker than with hallowing His name? Jesus places supreme priority on the holy things surrounding God's name, making the first petition a plea against contemptuous or negligent use and a prayer that His people use it holily. They must hold it in high estimation, sanctifying it in their hearts

---

[5] Lancelot Andrewes, Scala Cœli Nineteen Sermons Concerning Prayer. (London: N. Okes, 1611), 124.

so others may see their holy light. This prayer extends beyond personal holiness to include others, which is why they pray, "Our Father who art in heaven, hallowed be thy name..."

Those who would see God's name hallowed and glorified must approach Him with earnest seriousness in prayer. What gravity ought *we* to bring to sanctifying God's name? Christ deemed it not merely a daily prayer but the first and principal one you are to offer each day. In such prayer, you manifest and acknowledge God's holiness, for His holiness is the beauty and splendor of His attributes, which you are to adore. His greatness and brilliance shine forth in His holiness: "...great is the Holy One of Israel in the midst of thee," (Isa. 12:6). The angels, as we have noted, ceaselessly cry out, "holy, holy, holy," and so should you: "Who is like thee, glorious in holiness," (Exod. 15:11).

What, then, do you desire when you pray? How have your prayers been shaped thus far? Is holiness their center, that the Father's holy name be glorified in the reverent use of His titles, attributes, words, and works by you? You cannot truly be a subject of God's Kingdom or do His will unless, as Christ prioritizes, you exercise your thoughts, yourself, and your brethren in holiness—the principal account you render of the Father's glory. What do you rush to prayer for first? Many seek honor, riches, profit, or pleasure—perhaps a new weed-whacker—dishonoring God and disregarding His holiness thereby.

In prayer, you seek God's bestowals, but in this first petition, Christ directs you *to crave holiness*. Why? Because only God, through His Holy Spirit, can grant sanctification. No one can hallow God's name apart from the Spirit's work. Profane people and devils may glorify God unwillingly, but only those called children of the Father, made holy by Christ Jesus, can sanctify His name. The angels proclaim, "Holy, holy, holy is the Lord God of hosts, the whole earth is full of thy glory," and the four beasts in Revelation rest not, declaring, "Holy, holy, holy Lord God Almighty, which was and is, and is to come." On Aaron's breastplate and forehead bands was inscribed, "Holiness to the Lord." Where, then, shall you seek this holiness? At the ark, the throne of grace at Christ's feet, under His mercy's wings. You must resort to the fountain of holiness for the grace of separateness, that He may sanctify you to sanctify His name in Christ.

When we pray, "hallowed be thy name," we desire not only that God's name be hallowed by us but in us—that He enlighten us with the knowledge of His holiness, pressing His holy name deeper into us, drawing us closer. This petition acknowledges our utter inability and indisposition, and that of all men, to honor God aright. We pray that by grace we be enabled to know, acknowledge, and highly esteem Him in His titles, attributes, ordinances, Word, and works, glorifying

Him in thought, word, and deed in all He reveals Himself by. We ask that He remove ignorance, idolatry, profaneness, and all dishonor to Him, directing all things by His providence to His glory. This is the daily prayer of believers who follow Christ's instruction, seeking true knowledge of His holiness, heartfelt daily prayer, true faith, repentance, and renewal by His Spirit to be holy as He is. Zacharias Ursinus wrote, "That he would give us a disposition to profess this holiness of his divine name in word and deed, to his own praise and glory, that we may in this way glorify him by acknowledging and professing him, and by conforming our lives to his holy will, so as to distinguish him from all idols and profane things."[6]

As with the commandments, the Lord's Prayer's petitions carry opposites to consider. In praying for hallowing, you seek freedom from spiritual pride and corruptions opposing God, that your heart not be hardened but pliable to heed His will in a holy manner, not unthankful for His mercies, nor set in ungodliness and sin, never reproaching His name.

Yet there are positives too. You petition for God's name to be hallowed, desiring deeper knowledge of Him in grace—more of Christ, His sweet words, delight,

---

[6] Zacharias Ursinus and G. W. Williard, *The Commentary of Dr. Zacharias Ursinus on the Heidelberg Catechism* (Cincinnati, OH: Elm Street Printing Company, 1888), 631.

repose, and holiness. Through Christ, God reveals Himself for intimate fellowship, your very life. How can you glorify God *without knowing Him*? Young converts glorify God, certainly, but what of mature, learned Christians? You petition this hallowing with zeal for God's glory, tied to His holiness. As Psalm 69:9 says of Christ, "Zeal of thine house hath eaten me up." How many Christians are *consumed with zeal* for God's holiness and worship? You petition this hallowing for the church's people and your own godly walk, desiring to walk in sincerity and holiness, as God's majesty demands. Are you Abraham's children? God told Abraham, "...walk before me, and be thou perfect," (Gen. 17:1), and of his household, "For I know him, that he will command his children and his household after him, and they shall keep the way of the LORD," (Gen. 18:19). That way is to walk worthy of the Lord, honoring "our Father" who reigns in heaven. You petition not merely to know God but to advance cheerfully in professing His truth and worshiping His name—your life—desiring not to pollute but to magnify it. This extends to your brethren, that they too sanctify God's name, so others may say, "God is in you of a truth," (1 Cor. 14:25). You desire this in the highest, for all. Men naturally chase temporal things for happiness, but your duty as a Christian is to ascribe all glory to the Father through holy worship: "Not unto us, O LORD, not unto us, but unto thy name give glory, for thy mercy, and for thy truth's sake," (Psa.

115:1). By fervently praying to hallow God's name here, you will one day join the angels of Isaiah 6, ceaselessly proclaiming His holiness.

This petition also carries, by implication, a missionary mindedness. We pray that God, glorious in Himself, may be declared and made known to men. You may wonder, is this not the preacher's task? Yet we pray that His wisdom, power, mercy, and grace be increasingly imparted into us and others of "our" Father in the church, that the fruits of these may appear in people's lives, so God's name may be honored and praised by all who behold the light. We pray that ignorance of holy things be dispelled, that we and others come to a holy knowledge of His titles, attributes, ordinances, Word, and works, desiring good and holy works by which God is glorified in us through Christ and the Spirit's power. We pray that all falsehood, wickedness, and ungodliness—by which God's name is dishonored—be abolished in His people, and that His holiness shine brightly in His titles, attributes, ordinances, Word, and works.

Consider an outline for your first petition in prayer. You are to be stirred with excitement for personal holiness above all else, desiring to cultivate it, asking God to kindle this zeal in your whole being. Is He not a holy God and just Judge? You know no man is innocent in His sight, none are free from sin's stain.

You have no glory to bring to judgment, stripped of innocence's covering needed before God. You fall hourly, seventy times seven daily. The spirit may be willing, but the flesh remains weak. The inward man flourishes, yet the outward languishes. You persist in what you hate, contrary to holiness. Vain, wicked, impious thoughts arise often; unprofitable, hurtful words escape your lips or mind; perverse, ungodly actions defile you. All your righteousness is as filthy rags. In this way, you dare not plead your righteousness before God. Humbly, you approach His judgment seat, crying from your heart: "Lord, if you shall decree to impute sin, who shall abide it? If you will enter into judgment, who shall stand? If you call me to appear according to the severity of your justice, how shall I come before you? If you exact a strict account of my life, I shall not be able to answer you one for a thousand. Therefore my mouth is stopped, and I acknowledge before you, that I have deserved eternal torments; and with this I confess that you may justly cast me into prison for ever." What can you offer Him that is holy? "Therefore, for these daily sins of my life, I offer to you (holy Father) *the most precious blood of your Son*, which was poured forth on the altar of the cross, which washes me from all my sins. My sins which lead me captive, are many in number, and most powerful. But the ransom of your Son Jesus Christ is much more precious, and of more efficacy because he is perfectly holy. Let that most perfect, complete, and holy price paid by Christ, obtain for me all I need before you."

You pray that holiness yields power—spiritual power, vitally connected to Christ, that you might draw virtue from Him. You pray that every work be brought to judgment, knowing all are, desiring a constraint in holiness, to honor God with reverence, to live constantly and victoriously in the Spirit, abundantly. You consider holiness in light of your sins, pondering what underlies the sins you seek to mortify, desiring aid to take their slaying seriously, to *don* Christ's holiness, reflecting His, making His name holy around and in you. "He who called you is holy, you also be holy in all your conduct, because it is written, 'Be holy, for I am holy,'" (1 Peter 1:15-16). You seek to be a good steward of holiness—heart, soul, and mind—reflecting Christ's holiness.

Here is a simple summary encapsulating this petition: "Hallowed be thy name" is a plea worthy of the children of such a Father as God. As His good children, their chief care is to seek and desire whatever honors their Father. Thus, in this first petition, we covet that God our Father be hallowed and sanctified in us—that He be known, honored, and reverenced by us. By His grace through Christ, we perform works that lead all who see us to praise and glorify our heavenly Father. You are zealously consumed with honoring Him, manifesting His honor in your life, yearning to see His Spirit work within you, rejecting all that dishonors Him.

What constitutes such dishonor in your life? This is what Christ expects you to embrace in the first petition. You seek grace for yourself and the church to sanctify and glorify Him as our Father reigning in heaven, praying for all needful graces to glorify Him in the world—the central aim of petitioning the throne of grace. This is what Jesus desires His disciples, preachers, and those sent into the world to hold foremost, separation from the world. You pray for knowledge and understanding of His nature, will, and works, for you cannot glorify an unknown God—yet how many attempt this in ignorance? You pray for grace to promote His honor, requiring spiritual strength, especially when the wicked and lukewarm professing Christian's rail against holiness, content in tepidity. You pray to give Christ the highest glory, aspiring to the greatest heights men can ascribe to Him, that your mouth be free of guile, filled with savory praise that ministers grace to hearers. You pray your works adorn holiness with a humble, blameless, exemplary life, glorifying your heavenly Father through good works.

Pray in this way: "O Lord God, may your name, your own glorious, and holy self, be praised by my love and honor of you, walking in the Spirit. Here I acknowledge my utter inability to honor you rightly. And that we would all be enabled by grace and inclined to know, to acknowledge, and highly to esteem you, in your titles, attributes, ordinances, word, and works as those most holy things we can know. That, whatever you are to make yourself known by, that we would in turn glorify you in thought, word, and deed. And that in us you would remove all ignorance, idolatry, profaneness, and whatsoever is dishonorable to you; and, by your overruling providence, direct and dispose of all things to your own glory. May your infinite goodness and greatness be forever, by all men and all angels, confessed, and admired, and adored, and magnified both in private and public, in our hearts, our mouths and our lives. May all creatures share in your goodness O God. Let all creatures help us to glorify your Name in holiness. And such is to say, with the psalmist, may everything that has breath, praise the Lord."

Do you see the vast scope of this first petition? It reaches to a myriad of branches and places, demanding that God's name be regarded as holy in His titles, attributes, ordinances, Word, and works in your life. In the next chapter, we will explore the *scope and manner* of living in His Kingdom.

Chapter 3: Thy Kingdom Come

Matthew 6:10, "Thy kingdom come."

Christ inaugurates the fullness of the Kingdom of God, the promised realities that will unfold through his death and resurrection, even before those events transpire in time. The essence of the Gospel, though bound to its mechanism, remains a present truth; the gospel of the kingdom of God is at hand, and it must be proclaimed for God, about God, and to the glory of God. The advent of the Kingdom of God and the gospel are one and the same; they herald the Gospel's mechanism because of its core message—that Our God Reigns. It is striking that God employs "our" in the Isaiah passage concerning the Gospel, as Paul expounds in Romans, and Christ echoes with "Our Father" in the prayer's opening.

As it pertains to the Christian's daily prayers, the petition for the kingdom's coming is positioned between the hallowing of Our Father's name—a daily plea for holiness, acknowledging the Father who reigns and can reverse the Fall as both Creator and Redeemer—and the subsequent call for obedience to His will, "thy will be done," (Matt. 6:9-10). The Kingdom resides in the midst, referring in both instances to the reigning Father in heaven. Men must hallow the Father's name and execute the King's will, for "Our God Reigns" is the Father's Gospel, all intertwined with sovereign rule. Between these lies the manner of living before the holy, reigning Father—the kingdom's advance in seizing this world, precisely what Christ bids his disciples to seek out in the Lord's Prayer.

In instructing his disciples to pray, Jesus orients their minds toward the one addressed filially as "our Father," emphasizing God's holiness, then the Spirit's work in fulfilling divine promises through the Kingdom, and obedience to His will. Post-resurrection, Christ appeared to commission them for the kingdom's expansion: "But ye shall receive power, after that the Holy Ghost is come upon you: and ye shall be witnesses unto me both in Jerusalem, and in all Judaea, and in Samaria, and unto the uttermost part of the earth," (Acts 1:8). This verse anchors the book of Acts and Christ's charge for the kingdom's growth, both physical and spiritual. Governed by the Spirit, the disciples were to extend the Gospel—"Our God Reigns"—to earth's farthest bounds, achieved when it reached Rome, the world's end. Imagine contemporary leaders presuming the apostles *failed*, urging global evangelism anew—not grasping that the apostles fulfilled Christ's word, nor the Gospel's essence. Aside from such, all Christ required for worldwide Gospel proclamation was accomplished, as Luke records: "Preaching the kingdom of God, and teaching those things which concern the Lord Jesus

Christ, with all confidence, no man forbidding him," (Acts 28:31).

The plea for the kingdom to come further entails believers' ongoing prayer for the Spirit of God's *fuller* influence—the entirety of Christ's spiritual blessings in the Christian—manifested daily by the Father's holy, sovereign power. The Lord's Prayer is a daily entreaty for this: a plea for each step, a lamp to one's path, day by day, to witness the kingdom's expansion through the Spirit; holiness to the Father is realized in kingdom influence, in Spirit-influence.

Most Christians err in interpreting this petition twofold. First, some suppose the kingdom has not yet encircled the globe or reached Christ's intended scope for unhindered preaching, erecting vast missionary apparatuses funded by millions, misconstruing not only Luke but Jesus Christ. They deem this prayer *missionary*, presuming the Christian community must now fulfill what apostles purportedly neglected. They overlook Acts' thrust. Second, others view the kingdom as distant, arriving only at Christ's return. They disregard texts proclaiming the kingdom and Christ's apostolic commission to herald God's holy reign.

Yet when Christ preached the kingdom, it was a present reality, "But if I with the finger of God cast out devils, no doubt the kingdom of God is come upon you," (Luke 11:20). Or, "From that time Jesus began to preach, and to say, Repent: for the kingdom of heaven is at hand," (Matt. 4:17)—proclaimed before His crucifixion or resurrection. What, then, binds to this "coming of the Kingdom"? "Thy kingdom come." If John the Baptist and Jesus could commence preaching the kingdom at hand, it presumes the concept was entrenched in hearers' minds. Jesus teaches this present kingdom, bidding disciples proclaim it and pray for its expansion without hint of misunderstanding, revealing vital kingdom principles—the contemporary church seems exceedingly ignorant of this.

The Jews awaited a Messiah on a white horse to crush Roman foes, missing Jesus through misconstrued redemption. They overlooked the holy Father's kingship in the Old Testament, His covenant through Messiah, earthbound in religious pursuits. Without Old Testament kingdom grounding, New Testament proclamation or prayer remains incomprehensible. Tied to this at-hand kingdom in Jesus' preaching is a daily prayer for its expansion in disciples' duties, and all believers via the Lord's Prayer. Christ's apostles were to preach it worldwide, empowered by Pentecost, a task fulfilled. Equally, believers pray daily for the kingdom to come... more. The kingdom is now and not yet: ushered fully by Christ, yet incomplete until His exaltation and return, consummate all in kingship. Acts' events herald the gospel's spread and Pentecost's power, manifesting the kingdom. What connects to disciples' kingdom expansion, warranting daily prayer? Merely for others?

For *missionary* ventures? These disciples evince the kingdom's further unveiling—God's end-time rule through Christ—in effective prayer. The Spirit, given maximally, empowers the church for service with Christ in heaven. Jesus works in believers through the Spirit, baptized therein, rendered kingdom-serviceable. What, then, to consider herein?

Doctrine: To pray for the Kingdom to come is to pray for the Holy Spirit to come *by degrees*, increasing His influence and power in the lives of Christ's disciples. Who is the supreme gift given by Christ from above? Is it not the Holy Spirit—a *holy* Spirit, perpetuating the Father's desire to hallow His name in believers' lives through holiness for worship? The Holy Spirit is the paramount endowment God bestows upon His children in answer to their prayer, "Thy Kingdom come." To pray for the Kingdom is to pray for the Spirit. But has He not already extensively come in Acts 2? He is a wondrous gift, the sensible essence of prayer for every believer, enabling prayer in the Spirit, by the Word, experienced with the influence and power it ought to embody. As Jesus declares, "If ye then, being evil, know how to give good gifts unto your children: how much more shall your heavenly Father give the Holy Spirit to them that ask him?" (Luke 11:13). This simple thought transforms all Christian prayer into a daily pursuit.

This promise ties to the Lord's Prayer in Luke 11. The Spirit's gift undergirds all Jesus taught His disciples to pray. The Holy Spirit authors the *application* of Christ's kingdom work: the Gospel's essence is revealed through the Father's sending of Christ to satisfy divine justice, extended by the Spirit's sanctifying work in expanding the Kingdom. The Spirit dispenses salvation's gifts and kingdom service among God's people, serving as the conduit for the Father and Son to indwell believers alongside Himself. He fosters communion between Father, Son, and His people, acting as another Comforter, a legal Advocate aiding believers in sanctifying God's name and fulfilling His will on earth. As the prayer unfolds, the Spirit sustains believers' temporal necessities, freeing them from fear of lacking daily bread, grants certainty of repentance and forgiveness for sins, and empowers them as soldiers in Christ's army against the devil's wiles, shielding them from the Evil One—the final three petitions.

Jesus, the Messiah, was furnished by the Father in *covenant* with an *immeasurable* filling of the Holy Spirit, bestowing that power from heaven into believers' lives upon conversion. The Spirit's gift results from the Kingdom's coming, and praying for it to come more seeks greater influences of the Kingdom through the Spirit's power. Who recites the Lord's Prayer with this in mind? This demands a practical turn: the Kingdom and Spirit are established initially in the heart, with subsequent effects in sanctification.

The Kingdom of Christ, the Kingdom of God, is established by the Spirit in the heart: "The kingdom of God is within you," (Luke 17:21). It is "not eating and drinking—but righteousness, peace, and joy in the Holy Spirit," (Romans 14:17). The Kingdom (second petition) is holiness (first petition). Before Christ's kingdom reigns in a heart, the kingdom of darkness holds sway, answerable to the Ten Commandments. Such individuals are under "the power of Satan" (Acts 26:18), captive "at his will" (2 Tim 2:26), loving *him* as a father instead of God. Those remaining in that kingdom face King Jesus' unimaginable wrath: "Thou, even thou, art to be feared: and who may stand in thy sight when once thou art angry?" (Psa. 76:7). In the end, wicked kings and men, rich and poor, call for rocks and mountains to hide them from His wrath (Rev 6:16). Two kingdoms govern men's hearts: darkness or light, Satan or God (Col. 1:13). By Adam's fall, men are subject to the kingdom of darkness under God's curse; yet, by representation, they may be translated into light in the Lord, endowed with new power.

In Satan's kingdom, the law is sin—lawlessness. Sin reigns in mortal bodies, making men instruments of wickedness (Rom. 6:12-13), aiming for endless punishment. But when God's kingdom comes upon His children, ruling by His Word and Spirit, they are saved, transformed into serviceable subjects, adopted into His family—the kingdom of God, imbued with the Spirit's influence. God universally rules all, even enemies, from His chariot throne with a rod of iron: "The LORD reigneth; let the people tremble: he sitteth between the cherubims; let the earth be moved. The LORD is great in Zion; and he is high above all the people," (Psa. 99:1-2). Christ's throne, established in heaven, governs irresistibly, unhindered by fools opposing Him.

Yet God's special kingdom, for which Christ bids disciples pray, rules not all men generally but the elect—His church, in two parts: the triumphant church in heaven (Revelation 14) and the militant church on earth, praying daily for what heaven's saints possess fully. The *militant* yields to the *glorious*, but entry into glory requires true membership *in* the militant church: "out of the church there is no salvation." Loving Jesus without loving His church is folly. True believers in the Father through His Son, in the kingdom of grace, shall inherit glory. This kingdom of grace is what disciples pray to come more—a government where the Lord rules hearts by His Word and Spirit, working grace, making them fellow-citizens and heirs of the saints' inheritance (Eph. 2:19; Col. 1:12). The Redeemer reigns by sovereign power through Word and Spirit, His people called the church, the kingdom of heaven (Matt. 5:19), comprising regenerated, Spirit-enlivened Christians and temporary visible church members. The kingdom's ruling scepter is

God's Word, which believers reach to touch, as a golden scepter—the law of Christ, the Gospel of the Kingdom (Matt. 13:19; Mark 1:14).

When the Kingdom comes, the Spirit transforms stone hearts into flesh through the regenerating Word preached, rendering believers serviceable to the King in mercy and grace. Carnal pursuits give way to spiritual ones, centered on serving the Father in holiness, in His kingdom, to do His will. They become brothers and sisters under a new Father, praying not selfishly—"my God"—but as "Our Father," mindful of others' interests, for all revolves around the King's active and passive work through the Spirit. As new creations, they receive and do good works for God's glory. This new Father, by creation and spiritual redemption, grants privileges unattainable to the wicked. Can a wicked man pray this? Impossible. God is their Father by creation, but not redemption until the Spirit impresses Christ's particular atonement, spurring the renewed to pray for the Kingdom's greater influence on their soul—not merely for "jungle missionaries." The renewed Christian, delivered, desires the Father's will, knowing holiness encapsulates all through "Hallowed be thy Name." How will they experience this? How will they serve God in holiness? Their darkness dispelled by God's power, they pray for more to manifest in their walk: "Thy Kingdom come" more in me.

The preaching of the Word and Gospel is the kingdom of heaven (Matt. 13:11, 22). Where the Gospel is *truly* preached, *there* is the kingdom, and therefore the Father's church. By this Word, the Spirit rules hearts, drawing them to the Son, bending them to obedience, enlightening minds, renewing hearts, leading to truth. This mortifies sin (first petition) and renews in holiness daily (second petition). The kingdom's end is glory: "Fear not, little flock; for it is your Father's good pleasure to give you the kingdom," (Luke 12:32)—covenant privileges in Spirit-influence. God pulls His people from darkness into grace by His Word and Spirit, granting remission of sins and an inheritance among the sanctified (Acts 26:18), "everlasting life" (John 5:24), destined for glorification with the elect (Rom. 8:30). The Kingdom's coming in Spirit-power entails destroying the devil's power (Rev. 12:9, 10), delivering captives (Luke 4:18), gathering God's people to serve, glorify, and enjoy Christ (Acts 15:14; Eph. 1:10; 1 Pet. 2:9), and making His church glorious, universal, and perfect in holiness, (Mal. 1:11; Rom. 10:12; Eph. 5:26, 27), accomplished by spiritual influences (John 16:4–11; 2 Cor. 10:4). This kingdom's coming is not its inauguration, as Hodge notes: "The kingdom of grace began with the first promise in Gen. 3:15, was renewed in the family of Abraham (Gen. 12:1–3), was made a power among the nations under Moses (Exod. 3:6–10), and was developed as spiritual and universal as the 'kingdom of heaven,' by

Christ (Matt. 4:16, 17; John 18:36, 37)."[7] Disciples pray for its powerful coming and ultimate consummation as the kingdom of glory (Matt. 25:34; 26:64; Luke 22:16), yearning to taste it now, be furthered in it, and to see the Spirit's influence dominate the church and their lives.

How might this petition be summarized to grasp what one is to pray for in it? First, that Satan's kingdom may be destroyed. Satan, the avowed foe of God's kingdom, may be overthrown; and all sin's power in a believer and fellow believers—by which Satan holds sway—may be subdued. "Let God arise, let his enemies be scattered: let them also that hate him flee before him," (Psa. 68:1). "He that committeth sin is of the devil. For this purpose the Son of God was manifested, that he might destroy the works of the devil," (1 John 3:8). Believers crave no share in this, yearning for sin's subjugation by the Spirit's power and the Word's rule. What does the coming of God's kingdom signify in subduing darkness? It removes all hindrances, manifesting the Gospel of the Kingdom in believers and to the world: "Finally, brethren, pray for us, that the word of the Lord may have free course, and be glorified, even as it is with you," (2 Thess. 3:1). Who obstructs the Gospel? In Acts, the devil, wicked men and their lusts, and Antichrist—the man of sin—impede, some more

---

[7] Archibald Alexander Hodge, *The System of Theology Contained in the Westminster Shorter Catechism: Opened and Explained.* (New York: A. C. Armstrong and Son, 1888), 160–161.

visibly than others. This petition stands in direct opposition to the devil's efforts to thwart the Spirit's work, or his attempts to do that, through faithful disciples *praying* for God's power to reign via the Spirit in themselves and those around them. In this way, Christ Jesus' kingdom expands by the Spirit's power and influence, through the Word. Darkness dissipates by the Spirit applying Christ's merit as Kinsman Redeemer and Avenger for His people. Does the Spirit accomplish this despite believers, or harness their prayers and Word-aligned works to vanquish evil deeds around and within them? This leads to the *second facet...*

Second, that the kingdom of grace and the Holy Spirit's power in His people may *advance*. Christians, in general, desire God's kingdom of grace to advance worldwide, praising the Son above all other realms: "And it shall come to pass in the last days, that the mountain of the Lord's house shall be established in the top of the mountains, and shall be exalted above the hills, and all nations shall bow unto it," (Isa. 2:2). Christians in particular, and others, may be drawn into this kingdom of grace by God's power and Spirit in their conversion: "The Gentiles to whom I now send thee, to open their eyes, and to turn them from darkness to light, and from the power of Satan unto God," (Acts 26:17-18). For those already in the kingdom of grace through the Spirit and baptism therein, grace may strengthen and establish them: "The God of all grace, who hath called us unto his eternal glory by Christ Jesus, after that ye have suffered a while, make you perfect, stablish, strengthen, settle you," (1 Peter 5:10). What does it mean that the *kingdom's coming,* if not the Holy Spirit's influences overwhelming God's people? They pray for its manifestation, propagation, and perfection in themselves and their church. Those truly desiring God's name hallowed will pray for His kingdom to come in the Spirit's power, for the Spirit alone fosters holiness. This petition invokes Satan's kingdom's destruction, advancing God's power in believers. How many spiritual applications arise here for subverting idolatrous worship of every kind and degree, destroying it through the Spirit's work via disciples and the Word, while dispelling Satan's influences in the world? Here, the kingdom of grace advances by the Spirit in disciples—not merely established and exalted, but rightly exercised in duties owed to Christ and particular people. King Jesus may receive crowns at His feet, yes; the kingdom and its spiritual influences expand in believers and the church to the world, yes; the Spirit pours out plentifully with greater influence, yes; the Spirit converts more, bringing men savingly to Christ, yes. But Christ's laws and ordinances in His Word must be obeyed by His people: professing Christians subject to Him in all; order in His church, orderly walking before the Father in worship, by the Spirit's power. His authority glorified, His fear dwelling in the hearts of His people by the

Spirit—they pray for more such influence. They desire fidelity to Him, praying against apostasy from the church. The Spirit subdues hearts, rooting out carnal opposition, reigning by His Word and Law in the church. Christians today scarcely consider this, perhaps never hearing it before.

Yet another dimension must not be overlooked: the kingdom of glory's finality may hasten to come *swiftly*. Regarding the kingdom of glory, Christ's return to consummate and finalize His kingdom would arrive quickly: "Surely I come quickly. Amen. Even so, come, Lord Jesus," (Rev. 22:20). Though believers pray for the kingdom's expansion within them and the Spirit's fuller manifestation, they keep in view its hastening finality (they *desire* that hastening). This is the day of the Lord, when Christ returns to judge the world and complete His covenant work of exaltation. Believers must anticipate, wait for, and delight in this day, where Christ is exalted supremely. Christ directs prayer for kingdom influence now and eager expectation of its fullness in the future. All His people pray particularly for one another, that His elect be fitted for the King's coming and kingdom's finalization. Christ would gather all His elect. By the Spirit, He advances His promises toward accomplishment, bringing the kingdom's consummation—for praying for the kingdom to come is praying for the Holy Spirit to come by degrees in His influence and power in the lives of Christ's disciples.

The petition surrounds the influences of the Spirit in your life. If this petition centers on the Holy Spirit's work in your life, how will you pray for the Spirit's influence in the coming of the Kingdom upon you? What *words* will you employ? Here, Christ directs all disciples to pray for the coming of His Spirit's influences: "thy kingdom come." This teaches them to seek the practical and powerful application of His work, worked through the Spirit, into His people's lives. How many facets does this encompass? Are you overwhelmed, contemplating "Our Father" and all that holiness entails, now compounded by the Spirit's influence in your life? And we have yet to reach God's will or daily necessities. As the commandments divide between duties to God and neighbor, so the prayer you offer respects first God and His work, then you. To pray this prayer is to believe in Christ's death and resurrection, for the Spirit's gift ties directly to Christ's exaltation. How few Christians truly desire God's glory as this petition manifests; how few grasp it? No wonder the Westminster Catechisms pair the Lord's Prayer with the Ten Commandments as directives. What do you do to expand the Kingdom in the Spirit's power? This petition concerns not only glorifying God in His kingdom through the Spirit but also your happiness therein. Satan's kingdom and sin must be subdued around and in you; the Spirit guides you by the Word, to which you willingly submit with a new heart as a new creation in Christ Jesus. Christ deserves the Kingdom—He rules as King, earned as Mediator, and will see His soul's travail fulfilled in its fullness through the Spirit's work in His subjects, including you as a professing Christian. In His kingdom, under His kingship, lies your true happiness, to be fully realized in the Kingdom of Glory. When that Kingdom comes in fullness, Christ will appear in glory, and you will reign with Him forever. Therefore, set yourself prayerfully against scoffers of godliness and holiness, and those who rest in mere form, denying its power (2 Tim. 3:5). Such are true persecutors of religion—not only those who kill or martyr, but those subverting truth, tempting others to deny the Spirit's kingdom influence in your daily walk. How many professing Christians do this?

Be exhorted to sanctify God's Name by praying to promote Christ's Kingdom in the Spirit. Does this not lend fresh meaning to Christ's words: "seek ye first the kingdom of God, and his righteousness; and all these things shall be added unto you," (Matt. 6:33)? What things? Repeatedly, Christ directs His people to the Spirit's work in their lives—by law, practice, word, deed, holiness, influence. Seeking first the kingdom means praying for the expansion of the Spirit's influence in your life. As Samuel Willard noted, "Prayer that is right, will not be contradicted by practice."[8]

When Christ taught us to pray, "Thy Kingdom come," He aimed for His Kingdom to expand through the Spirit's power in you and for its swift consummation (though *we don't know* when that will be). One cannot be a true Christian without desiring Christ's kingdom to come—Christ as King, appearing in glory to judge the world, and the Spirit's influence fostering holiness. You have great reason to crave this day: it will bring vengeance on your enemies for wrongs done, final pardon for your sins, and salvation for your soul (Hebrews 9:28). What begins here will be perfected at Christ's glorious appearing, saving you to the uttermost. You must understand "kingdom"—the Father's, God's, Christ Jesus' *kingdom.* As God's name is holy yet we pray it be hallowed among us, so the kingdom comes, and we pray for its coming in the Spirit's power to partake in hallowing God's name. We pray God's kingdom comes to us, His will done in us, subjecting us to Christ's kingship. Without King Jesus, what is a kingdom? He is the king of righteousness and life against the devil, sin, death, and evil conscience. He gives His holy Word to be preached, that we believe and live holy lives by the Spirit's grace—not merely existing in light, but walking

---

[8] Samuel Willard, *A Compleat Body of Divinity* (Boston in New-England: B. Green and S. Kneeland for B. Eliot and D. Henchman, and sold at their shops, 1726), 909.

in it as He is in it. Pray that this King, sending His Spirit, becomes effective and powerful in you, that the Word goes forth with power from the church, that many enter this kingdom, believing, redeemed from death, sin, and hell's dark kingdom, translated into light. God's name must not be blasphemed but hallowed, honored, glorified by you, bearing fruit through the Spirit for your soul's good. How many petitions stem from this? Is it mere mimicry of "Our Father"? No, He desires you bear fruit in the Spirit, hallowing His name, manifesting His kingdom in us through the Word, securing eternal life. Calvin defines this petition thus: "God reigns when men, in denial of themselves and contempt of the world and this earthly life, devote themselves to righteousness and aspire to heaven."[9] Aspiring to heaven surpasses mere hope; it demands work.

How, then, do you employ means for the Spirit to be experienced and expanded in you, as in Christ's kingdom's influence? The Word of God is Christ's royal golden scepter; touch the top of it to find grace in need and direction for every step. Through the Word, by the Spirit, Christ subdues your mind and heart to voluntary obedience. The Spirit unveils the Word's efficacy, raising it to its deserved honor, as Calvin notes: What is this place? It is to be highly esteemed in practice and prayer—praying in the Spirit, by the Word, exercising

---

[9] John Calvin, *Institutes of the Christian Religion* (Bellingham, WA: Logos Bible Software, 1997) 3.20.42.

it, knowing how to pray it, so influenced that you pray the Word itself.[10]

In this prayer, you wield the principal means to sanctify God's name among you: the coming of His Kingdom, which is to say, the coming of His Spirit in you now. When the Spirit's power manifests and becomes evident, all aspects of the kingdom of grace come to you—either begun and established or continued and increased within you.

You are the subject of the King. A kingdom, broadly, is a government or state where Christ rules and you are ruled. By what will you be governed? Many today seek rule by what feels good, equating pleasant emotions with the Spirit's work—goosebumps or excitement mistaken for His presence. Yet the Kingdom's coming, the Spirit's influence and spiritual persuasion, hinges on looking to His power and guidance for eternal happiness through the Spirit's work in the Word within you. There Christ is found; there, under the Apple Tree, you repose and find Him delightful, daily.

The Kingdom's coming signifies motion for you, akin to walking from one place to another. As you consider the Spirit's motion in the Kingdom's work—in your heart, life, church, and world—you find matters to pray for and tasks to undertake. Pray that the Gospel,

---

[10] Ibid.

the Kingdom's golden scepter, be published and grow in your life; that those around you, in your household, conform more to the Gospel or be converted by it; that the Spirit's accompanying graces, His fruit, increase in and through you; and that all hindrances to your walk before Him be subdued. In this way, you pray for this Kingdom to expand greatly in Spirit-influence. At this juncture, you may feel overwhelmed by the myriad thoughts tied to this petition alone—first the Father, then holiness, now the Kingdom's Spirit-influence. This recurs because many fail to learn prayer rightly, and its depth overwhelms when we neglect its knowledge. Christ's Kingdom advances by degrees, a growing Kingdom you are to seek primarily—the Spirit, His guidance, His direction, His glorification of Christ in you. Does this not echo the Apostle's words: "I will pray with the spirit, and I will pray with the understanding also," (1 Cor. 14:15)?

Consider the Spirit's work in the Kingdom's coming: His influence on your soul, the degrees of holiness you possess or lack, the church's expansion, the removal of spiritual hindrances, the perfection of purity and holiness, the powerful dispensation of gospel-ordinances attended by the Spirit's efficacious work—is this not overwhelming? Pray therefore in this light: "O King of Kings, may your Kingdom of Grace, the church militant, that school of divine love, come to its greatest degree in this life, in my life. O may your Gospel, Lord, be propagated daily, unbelieving nations converted and the number of your saints increased by the greatness of your Spirit's influence in the world and the church. Grant, but let it be that your word, O Lord God, that your true religion, your word, your grace, all the holy institutions, laws and governors, fixed by you in your spiritual Kingdom, may be loved, and honored, and obeyed by me: and that I along with your faithful subjects may be protected against all the malice of wicked men, and the powers of darkness. O my God, let it be your good pleasure to put an end to sin and misery in me, to infirmity and death in me; to complete the number of your elect, and to hasten your Kingdom of glory that we, and all that wait for your salvation, may in the church triumphant eternally love and praise you. Make your Spirit to dominate my life and the life of others around me in your Kingdom now. That I and they may be more influenced by your Spirit as it regards the coming of more holiness to the honor and hallowing of the Father."

To pray for the Kingdom to come is to pray for the *sensible experience of the Holy Spirit to work by way of influence and power in your life.*

In the next chapter, we will consider God's *will* in our life.

Chapter 4: Thy Will Be Done

Matthew 6:10, "Thy will be done in earth, as it is in heaven."

The words of this text are aptly translated, presenting a contrast. God's will is to be done upon the earth as it is in heaven, where His will is accomplished with perfection in a world of love. The petition itself is "thy will be done in earth," measured against its flawless execution, "as it is in heaven." What will of God is intended here? This does not refer solely to His will of decree—the ordination and accomplishment of His wise purposes, which resides solely within Himself, impervious to any prayer's influence: "The things of God knoweth no man but the Spirit of God," (1 Cor. 2:11). Prayer, regarding His decree, merely aligns with it, provided it is not offered *amiss.*

In this instance of the Lord's Prayer, the focus is God's revealed will, or will of precept, as expressed in His commandments. Herein lies great peril for many Christians, who falter in ignorance of His commandments, their enduring relevance, their authority over them, and what the Father demands. In heaven, saints and angels fulfill His revealed will perfectly. Angels, lacking a Bible, are guided by the Spirit as ministering spirits, performing God's will *without question, excuse, or delay*. Saints in heaven, transformed by Christ upon entry, are equipped to do God's will flawlessly, without hesitation or hindrance.

This third petition, fitting seamlessly after the first two, is uttered by those on earth, beseeching the Father, by His grace, to make them able and willing to know, obey, and submit to His will in all things, as angels and saints do in heaven. *The 1647 Westminster Catechism* captures it thus: "What do we pray for in the third petition? Answer: In the third petition, which is, Thy will be done in earth, as it is in heaven, we pray, that God, by his grace, would make us able and willing to know, obey, and submit to his will in all things, as the angels do in heaven." John Cassian noted, to pray "Thy will be done in earth, as it is in heaven" is to pray that men may emulate angels, fulfilling God's will on earth as angels do in heaven, forsaking their own desires.[11]

The substance of the petition, "Thy will be done," specifies two circumstances: the place—earth, indicating the people, men; and the manner, set in comparison, "as it is in heaven." The matter is God's will, distinct from all others—men's or the devil's. The Father's will concerns His people's active obedience to His laws and commands, while they remain wholly

---

[11] CONFERENCES 9.20.1. Peter Gorday, ed., Colossians, 1–2 Thessalonians, 1–2 Timothy, Titus, Philemon, Ancient Christian Commentary on Scripture (Downers Grove, IL: InterVarsity Press, 2000), 156.

passive to His providence. They experience providence—rich or poor, healthy or sick—at God's discretion, but do not control it. They show obedience by praying to fulfill His will as revealed in His Word, which they must know and believe. They submit to His providence, with Scripture expressing their subjection in ways agreeable to His revealed will. They not only obey actively but love Christ's commandments, desiring their hearts be lifted to the King by the Spirit's influence in holiness, so the Father's desires become theirs increasingly, day by day.

Doctrine: The Christian prays daily that the Father's will would be their will; and that His will would be done in them universally, joyfully, constantly, humbly, thankfully, steadfastly, and promptly, as the angels and saints in heaven do.

The third petition teaches that the Father's great will, embodied in His authoritative commandments—the perfect rule of all that is right, displaying His character—is worthy and commanded to be obeyed perfectly by all on earth, as in heaven: "Bless the LORD, ye his angels, that excel in strength, that do his commandments, hearkening unto the voice of his word," (Psa. 103:20). Christians demonstrate their duty before God by accomplishing His will universally, joyfully, constantly, humbly, thankfully, steadfastly, and promptly, as heaven's angels and saints do. Christ's will is their duty; it is just and necessary that all creatures obey and conform to it. The first sin in the garden was failing to do what God commanded as He commanded. Christians, considering themselves and others, desire that the Lord allow His secret will to unfold per His pleasure, to which they submit, and that His revealed will be accomplished by His people and all creatures in like manner—universally, joyfully, constantly, humbly, thankfully, steadfastly, and promptly. They pray that all obstacles—stubborn, uncircumcised hearts, and all displeasing sin and disobedience—be eradicated from them and the world. Their hope, exercising His law, finds comfort in its fulfillment, though less perfectly here, growing by degree, yet they long for it to be done as it is in heaven. Having prayed for the Father to rule them as King in a filial, holy relationship, revering His name by the Spirit's power, they now seek a pliable heart to be ruled willingly by His Word and Spirit according to His perfect rule.

What is this *will* of God but *His commandments?* His decrees cannot be the petition's focus, for His will of purpose is always perfectly accomplished within Himself. God's purpose *is* His will; whatever He proposes, He wills and executes: "God from all eternity did, by the most wise and holy counsel of his own will, freely and unchangeably ordain whatsoever comes to pass."[12] He determines *absolutely* what shall be and what

[12] 1647 Westminster Confession of Faith 3:1.

shall not, through His Mediator and Son, governing all in the world and church—ruling with a rod of iron or from His mercy seat: "God worketh all things according to the counsel of his own will," (Eph. 1:11). This secret will, irresistible and invariably fulfilled, includes even the most heinous acts, like Christ's crucifixion: "Him, being delivered by the *determinate counsel and foreknowledge of God*, ye have taken, and by wicked hands have crucified and slain," (Acts 2:23). Though ordained by God's will, the Jews' voluntary wickedness rendered them guilty of history's gravest sin. Yet this secret will is not the saints' direct concern in this petition. They focus on conforming to the image of the only begotten Son through the precepts God has revealed clearly, without trickery. Those endowed with Kingdom influence, desiring holiness and loving the Father, are taught all things by the Spirit through the Word.

The Father's will of precept, written for the good and blessedness of rational men, is the will of God to which this petition points. It concerns men's duty: "the good, and acceptable, and perfect will of God," (Rom. 12:2). Contained in Scripture, it is Christ's perfect will, His law, guiding men's lives as they fulfill the cultural mandate to take dominion on earth. Christians pray daily that this will of precept be done, not only by themselves but by others, as the rule of their obedience, shaping all actions in character and conduct—universally, joyfully, constantly, humbly, thankfully, steadfastly, and promptly, as heaven's angels and saints do. Lacking ability to do this alone, they pray daily for such strength from above, seeking to emulate heaven's perfect obedience, that God's holy will be effected in them by Spirit-influence to treat God as holy in all things. They rely on Christ's grace to fulfill His will.

Why pray this petition for *earth*? A great enemy—the corrupt heart—strives against God's will: "The Law is spiritual; but we are carnal, and sold under sin," (Rom. 7:14). Even in the best Christians, a law in their bodies wars against their minds' law, found in the Word's precepts. When they desire good, evil is present. They desperately need to pray that Christ's will be done in and around them by themselves and others, complying universally, joyfully, constantly, humbly, thankfully, steadfastly, and promptly, as in heaven. Christ strengthens them to obey His commandments, aligning their wills with King Jesus' will. Professing to be His people and praying for His Kingdom's coming, they pray "thy will be done," for the Kingdom centers on the King and His will—His Word as the scepter and law. If professing Christians pursue other hobbies, neglecting His will, they quietly—or not so quietly—condemn it, aligning with *crowds* of contemporary evangelicalism that *resist* Christ's rule. Sincere believers strive to obey His commands, praying to do so universally, joyfully, constantly, humbly, thankfully, steadfastly, and promptly, pleasing and glorifying Christ as Prophet, Priest, and King. In this, they acknowledge the Kingdom, its King, its Spirit, its holiness, and the Father's joy in His titles, attributes, ordinances, words, and works.

This petition emphasizes "Thy will" be done—not any will, but the Father's in Christ, favored above all others: "Whether we ought to obey men rather than God, judge ye," (Acts 4:19). Is not the church's weekly prayer to rest in Christ's Word's protection? The Father's will, perfect and holy, is commanded as "hallowed be thy name" and "thy will be done." Exclusive, narrow, and constraining, it is deemed old-fashioned by some, yet teaches self-denial in all things. Failing to do His will—or worse, ignoring or partially obeying it when known—is rebellion. Men, fallen and cursed in vain imaginations, are contrasted with Christians who pray daily for submission to the Father's will over base lusts or Satan's will, renouncing both to do His will universally, joyfully, constantly, humbly, thankfully, steadfastly, and promptly. Christians long for meaningful lives, ordered in holiness, following the Father's will—the road to happiness, paved by God's Word.

Consider the comparison, "as it is in heaven." Can Christians do the Father's will on earth *as* in heaven? Does His glorious kingdom come here? They pray in degrees, "Thy kingdom come"—more influence, power, Spirit. Possessing grace now, they crave glory, desiring to do God's will as heaven's saints, though hindered and unable to fully achieve it. Yet they persist, refusing to give the Father rest until their prayers, aligned with His will, are answered in heaven, where they will do His will perfectly. Persevering eagerly, they avoid hypocrisy, for pursuing other ends betrays their profession. They cannot fully do God's will as in heaven, but true Christians do not use remaining sin as an excuse to neglect His commands. This prayer is not vain; it spurs them to aim for the perfect holiness of angels and just men made perfect, accomplishing God's will without challenge, excuse, or delay. Are they not commanded to be holy as God is, perfect as their Father is? They strive for higher holiness, pressed by heavenly rewards. What will they lose or gain? This earthly travail offers opportunity to conform to His image. Heaven's saints follow the Lamb whithersoever He goes (Rev. 14:4), their character marked by universal, joyful, constant, humble, thankful, steadfast, prompt obedience. Christians pray to emulate this temperament, seeking universal respect for all God's commandments, done with heaven's zeal. Earth is their journey to heaven, a trial ground, the sole place to exercise self-denial and obedience to Christ's will—a work begun here or never done.

In following His commandments, note that Christ is not the Christian's King when they pursue their own will. When Christians take exception to His

Word, they are hypocrites. When they misunderstand the Word, they hinder their walk. When they dismiss His commandments as antiquated or outdated, they fail to heed Christ's desire in this petition. By doing the Father's will, they enter His kingdom—see the connection? It is one thing for hypocrites to claim they follow Christ, but their sincerity is shown in doing His will. As James insists, words alone are insufficient; true faith manifests in outward conformity to the Word in character and conduct, for faith without holy works is dead. Jesus declares, "Not every one that saith unto me, Lord, Lord, shall enter into the kingdom of heaven; but he that doeth the will of my Father which is in heaven," (Matt. 7:21). It is not spiritual flattery Jesus seeks, but true subjection to His will of precept, which the Father deems good and necessary for His kingdom's subjects, even for entry therein. Christians must follow God's will over Satan's or their corrupted heart's.

This petition opposes, first, one's *own* will; second, *Satan's* will; and third, the wills of *men* in the world. In distinction to corruption, the perennial question of service to Christ the King is: whose will shall stand—the Father's or theirs? Sincere Christians know that all contrary to God's will is sin, insulting His commandments and elevating their own will, thereby affronting the King. In this way, they daily pray that God's will be done, relinquishing their own for the King's: "Let thy will be done as stated in your word, not our own." They pray their corrupt will be subdued to King Jesus. They also desire to do Christ's will against Satan's: "The lusts of your father the devil ye will do," (John 8:44). Wicked men, taken captive by Satan, obey him readily—universally, joyfully, constantly, steadfastly, and promptly, even in church. This prayer empowers believers to say, "Thy will, King Jesus, not the devil's," striving by Spirit-influence to be holy before the Father in all things. By extension, they desire "Thy will" over men's wills: "That he no longer should live to the lusts of men, but to the will of God," (1 Peter 4:2). Men do not dictate practice; the Word, through the Spirit, does—actively, pressingly, not magically in sleep. Have they sought God's will in Nahum, 2 Chronicles, or the Song of Songs?

To do the Father's will over their own, Satan's, or men's, Christians plead for a sound mind and heart to know and obey His Word: "Oh that there were such an heart in them, that they would fear me, and keep all my commandments always!" (Deut. 5:29). "Teach me to do thy will, for thou art my God," (Psa. 143:10). They pray King Jesus teach and lead them by Kingdom influence—more Holy Spirit, spiritual persuasion of the Word to inform mind and heart. Lacking ability themselves, they need resurrection power, looking to the Spirit's might: "The God of peace, through the blood of the everlasting covenant, make you perfect in every good work, to do his will," (Heb. 13:21). Why the heavenly comparison?

Christ avoids lowly examples, for people compare holiness relative to others—perhaps deeming pastors "professional Christians" holier than themselves. Jesus rejects this, setting heaven as the standard for all, especially ministers sent to preach His Gospel: "are you like angels and men made perfect?" Perfection, embodied in His commandments, is the Christian's aim, contrasted with heaven's flawless obedience, including Christ's own pattern: "Let this mind be in you, which was also in Christ Jesus," (Phil. 2:5).

Christians consider not only what they do (follow the Word) but how they do it (*thy kingdom come* by the Spirit). Christ teaches not just "Thy will be done," but "as it is in heaven." Do Christians ponder how their singing or service compares to heaven's? God examines not only the act but its manner, requiring universal, joyful, constant, humble, thankful, steadfast, prompt obedience—a tall order post-Fall. Excuses arise, "We are frail, imperfect; our submission is defective. How can we serve our King as heaven does?" God's will is *clear* from Genesis to Revelation, to be performed in Christ by the Spirit's power. Though imperfect, a likeness is achieved here through the Spirit's holy influence. Christians aim for perfection, praying and striving daily. Do they think His will is done on earth? Often, they act as if it is, yet pray vainly if they do not act. Jesus calls such hypocrisy: "This people draweth nigh unto me with their mouth, and honoureth me with their lips, but their heart is far from me," (Matt. 15:8). Unsuccessful prayers stem from *indifference*. When God commands His people to do His will and they lack heart, merely mouthing prayers like a rosary, what outcome awaits? James says they ask amiss. "If I be a father, where is mine honour? and if I be a master, where is my fear?" (Malachi 1:6). God questions those who profess Him but are not owned by Him: "Whosoever shall do the will of my Father which is in heaven, the same is my brother, and sister, and mother," (Matt. 12:50)—those who do His will are His kin. Thomas Manton noted, "Those that say, 'Our Father,' must also say, 'Thy will be done.'"[13] Otherwise, they wallow in gross hypocrisy, likely deceived about entering the Father's kingdom.

Respecting the Father's glory and His Son's Word requires doing His will, not merely professing it in ways pleasing to oneself. The Christian's subjection is to the Spirit's influence per the Word for the kingdom's glory and holy expansion. What is Christ as King without obedience to His law? Christ left an example: "I seek not mine own will, but the will of him that sent me," (John 5:30). He sought not His own will but the Father's as Mediator, fulfilling it universally, joyfully, constantly, humbly, thankfully, steadfastly, and promptly to the highest degree: "For Christ is the end of the law for righteousness," (Rom. 10:4). His people must

---

[13] Thomas Manton, *A Practical Exposition of the Lord's-Prayer* (London: J.D., 1684), 259.

love what He loves, hate what He hates, and follow His commands willingly, readily, faithfully. Those discarding Christ's holy law, thinking they can be Christians while libertines, face impossibility. Ecclesiastes concludes: "Fear God and keep his Commandments: for this is the whole duty of man." God will judge every work, secret or overt, good or evil. Knowing this, Christians are happy if they do it—their daily prayer that the Father's will be theirs, done universally, joyfully, constantly, humbly, thankfully, steadfastly, and promptly, as heaven's angels and saints do.

What is the Father's right over you? As a professing believer, consider His claim upon you. We are not at our own disposal but at the Lord's service. God holds a right over us as our Creator and Redeemer. The perfection of all creation lies in fulfilling His will, the end for which we were made. The chief end of man is God's glory, rooted in His will, for "all thy servants, and continue this day according to thine ordinances", (Psa. 119:91). We owe our being and all we have to Him. Christ the King has purchased you as a believer: "Glorify the Lord in your souls and bodies, which are God's," (1 Cor. 6:20). God owns you, not only in Christ but by granting you guidance to pray effectively per His prescription for your life. You cannot live as you please; you are God's property, His servant. Born from above by the Spirit, regenerated, what is the end of His grace? "That we should no longer live in the flesh, to the lusts of men, but to the will of God," (1 Peter 4:2). How often have Christians cited Song 7:10, "I am my beloved's"? Christians proclaim, "I am Christ's." How easy to say, but how are they to *show it*? Without *conscientious adherence to Christ the King's laws*, how can you claim Him? Some relish the idea of Christianity for its benefits, yet stand far from the Kingdom's Spirit-influence, showing no sincere respect for the Father or His commands found in the *Ten Commands* he laid down, transgressing His will without qualm. Their hearts neglect His ten commandments, of which *Scripture is a commentary*. To keep His will and pursue holiness, will they pray this petition sincerely? Justified by Christ, they need no other justification—but what of holiness? You are incapable of pleasing the Father alone. Your will must yield to King Jesus; His will is perfection, yours vain. As a Christian, be resolute to keep His will over your wayward one, holding His will in higher esteem. Is He not commanding? Is His will not holy and perfect?

To be given over to your own will is condemnation and judgment, a sign of reprobation, as Romans 1 warns: "Wherefore God also gave them up..." (Rom. 1:24). When God destroys a people, He surrenders them to their own will: "So I gave them up unto their own hearts' lust: and they walked in their own counsels," (Psa. 81:12). "Ephraim is joined to idols: let him alone," (Hosea 4:17). What is left to do? Many in the contemporary church struggle to do God's will broadly, endlessly asking, "What is God's will for my life?" yet resisting His commandments' yoke, mistaking it for bondage rather than liberty. They repeat the question, stuck in a scratched groove, finding no change. True liberty lies in submission to Christ's will in His Word: "If the Son therefore shall make you free, ye shall be free indeed," (John 8:36). Is this a passive act, done in sleep? No, it involves you, set at liberty to do His will in holiness and Kingdom expansion, by Spirit-influence. The more you do His will, the freer you find yourself in Him. Many mistake freedom for pursuing their own will, thinking highly of themselves.

Some presume that *professing love* for God earns a pass at judgment. Yet King Jesus will judge all done or left undone, punishing violations of His will to the degree deserved. He knows and records every work, intention, or rebellion, "The eyes of the Lord are in every place, beholding the evil and the good," (Prov. 15:3). James declares, "There is one lawgiver, who is able to save and to destroy," (James 4:12). Jesus warns, "but rather fear him which is able to destroy both soul and body in hell," (Matt. 10:28). Punishment aligns with His Word, intentions, and service—or violations thereof—measured by whether they did His will universally, joyfully, constantly, humbly, thankfully, steadfastly, and promptly, as heaven's angels and saints do.

As a Christian, surrender your will to do His. What is His will for you, for all? This prayer *ties* to His commandments. Be willing to obey God, whatever the cost, wherever He leads. Most flatter themselves with empty words, saying "Lord, Lord," their wills unresigned: "We will certainly do whatsoever thing goeth forth out of our own mouth," (Jer. 44:17). They think well of themselves, but Jesus demands sincerity: "And why call ye me, Lord, Lord, and do not the things which I say?" (Luke 6:46). Some oddly assume only Gospel sayings matter, not His full revealed will. Professing love without performing His will is empty. The Father seeks action—γίνομαι, "thy will be done," meaning to come into being, to be made real, preferred. Doing it partially, begrudgingly, sporadically, with murmuring, only on the Lord's Day, or with challenge is not universal, joyful, constant, humble, thankful, steadfast, or prompt, as heaven's saints do. Many shun knowing God's will or submitting to it, yet John 3:20 reveals the consequence: "Every one that doeth evil hateth the light, neither cometh to the light, lest his deeds should be reproved."

As a Christian, you are not only to pray daily that His will is done, but how it is done. Judas fulfilled God's secret will without ever adhering to His preceptive will, and he went to his own place. All your works must be performed with the full spiritual strength of a renewed heart, soul, and mind. When Christ evaluates what you have done or left undone, He weighs your actions and considers your disposition in doing them. How do you serve Him, how do you accomplish His will? Saying "Thy will be done" is not merely voicing or hoping for its fulfillment, but it concerns how you enact His will and what you contemplate while doing so. How do angels and saints serve Him in heaven, and how do you serve Him here, in this earthly life of trial? You are to serve Him universally, joyfully, constantly, humbly, thankfully, steadfastly, and promptly, as heaven's angels and saints do now.

A caution: you may grow despondent dwelling on this without praying as you ought. What will you offer the Father, whom you profess, desire to be holy for, and seek Spirit-influence to do His will, when you cannot do it as heartily as desired? You offer the works and ability of the Son on your behalf, striving to emulate, even faintly, the great pattern you long to see fulfilled in your life. How shall you do this? Is it merely reciting the prayer's words, or, as we have seen, embracing their expansive implications? Here is a prayer for this petition:

> "O my God, your will and your commands are most holy, just and good and condescending to our weakness, and by no mean grievous, give me grace to conscientiously observe them. Your blessed angels, Lord, always behold your face in

> heaven, and they have the beatific vision of your perfections and glory to behold, and they cannot but unalterably choose you. They must, of necessity to their utmost capacity praise and love you, they cannot possibly offend you, they ever perfectly obey you, and are always right there to do your bidding and will at your command. And so the saints too, stick close to you, and your atonement, that whithersoever you go they go. They are completely compliant in everything. Lord, give me grace, in imitation of the blessed spirits above, to set you always before me. Fix my adoration of you to be serious and careful according to your will. Ravish my soul with a lively sense of your infinite perfections. Promise me more glimpses of your goodness in your word. Allow the Spirit-influence of King Jesus to show me how gracious you are, that everything in the world besides you may be tasteless to me. Make my desires always be flying up towards you, that I may render to you love, and praise and obedience, pure and cheerful, constant and zealous, universal and uniform, like the holy angels and the saints in heaven render to you always."

In this and similar prayers, you seek to fulfill His will universally, joyfully, constantly, humbly, thankfully, steadfastly, and promptly, as heaven's angels and saints do now.

In the next chapter, we will consider the petition concerning *our daily bread.*

Chapter 5: Daily Bread

Matthew 6:11, "Give us this day our daily bread."

The verb δίδωμι, "to give," in the aorist active imperfect, implies giving an object of value. The term σήμερον, "today," denotes the same day as the prayer. The rare word ἐπιούσιος, used by Mark and later by Matthew and Luke, translates as "daily," meaning "necessary for existence," "for the current day," "for today," or "for the future," signifying what recurs daily. ἄρτος, "bread," indicates the prayer seeks God's provision of daily food for the coming day's needs. If prayed in the morning, it covers the day ahead; if in the evening, the next day—following the pattern of Exodus 16, where manna was given in the morning for *the day to come*. Yet, linked to the Kingdom's coming, this plea may also encompass the spiritual, eschatological bread promising lasting satisfaction. This prayer petitions Christ to supply food essential for life and being, addressing basic human need within the Kingdom prayer's framework. All prior requests—hallowing the Father's name, the Spirit's influence in the Kingdom's coming—now turn to daily sustenance, anticipating the Messianic feast in the Kingdom's fullness upon Jesus' return. The prayer's intent might be voiced this way:

"Deliver us, O Lord, from the fear of not having enough to eat. Give us bread for today and with it give us confidence that tomorrow we will have enough, with a willing expectation of the final eschatological feast we will have in the fullness of the Kingdom when Jesus returns."

After rendering due praise and respect to the Father, Christians are permitted and directed to request good things for themselves and their brethren. As the commandments enjoin loving God and neighbor as oneself, so does the Lord's Prayer. By this, they become capable of receiving and enjoying other blessings. They demonstrate total dependence on the Lord, needing daily bread as a gift from His hands, willingly relying on Him, casting all care upon Him, assured He cares for them, neither leaving nor forsaking them, nor withholding comfortable provisions. This implies moderation in both the quality and quantity of their desires. They seek only bread—the simplest, most common sustenance—necessary to maintain life and satisfy natural desires. Do Christians view the prayer this way? They learn to ask only for what sustains them: daily bread, a moderate provision when needed.

Doctrine: Christians are to pray that of God's free gift they may receive a competent portion of the good things of this life, and enjoy His blessing with them.

The fourth petition prompts Christians to acknowledge that, through Adam and their own sin, they have forfeited their right to this life's outward blessings, deserving to be wholly deprived of them by God and to have them cursed in use. *The 1647 Westminster Catechism* states: "Question 104. What do we pray for in the fourth petition? Answer: In the fourth petition, which is, Give us this day our daily bread, we pray that of God's free gift we may receive a competent portion of the good things of this life, and enjoy his blessing with them." Do Christians consider the *Fall* when praying this? Genesis 2:17 warns, "But of the tree of the knowledge of good and evil, thou shalt not eat of it: for in the day that thou eatest thereof thou shalt surely die." And he did die. The consequence? "Your iniquities have turned away these things, and your sins have withholden good things from you," (Jer. 5:25). A curse in the covenant's stipulation declares, "But it shall come to pass, if thou wilt not hearken unto the voice of the LORD thy God, to observe to do all his commandments and his statutes which I command thee this day; that all these curses shall come upon thee, and overtake thee: Cursed shalt thou be in the city, and cursed shalt thou be in the field. Cursed shall be thy basket and thy store," (Deut. 28:15-68). Using worldly things immoderately is part of this curse; continuing to use them sinfully perpetuates it.

Men, fallen and prone to immoderate desire, seek and use things unlawfully, needing reformation by the Spirit. When reformed in heart, soul, and mind, they adopt a new spiritual discipline, valuing the temporary lightly compared to the eternal. Christians pray for themselves and others, that all who call God Father wait on His providence daily, using lawful means. Once selfish and wicked, they now consider others' needs, exercising the commandment to love one another: "Give us this day our... daily bread." Biblically, men are often deplorable, driven by self-interest: "For from the least of them even unto the greatest of them every one is given to covetousness; and from the prophet even unto the priest every one dealeth falsely," (Jer. 6:13). "For from within, out of the heart of men, proceed evil thoughts, adulteries, fornications, murders, Thefts, covetousness, wickedness, deceit, lasciviousness, an evil eye, blasphemy, pride, foolishness," (Mark 7:21-22). But, renovated by the Spirit, transformed with new natures, they pray collectively for one another per the prayer's directive.

Christians receive life's necessities from the Father's hands in His wisdom, and they may enjoy a portion of such things, desiring their continuance and blessing for holy, comfortable use. This exemplifies the doctrine of *contentment*. Jacob confesses, "I am not worthy of the least of all the mercies, and of all the truth, which thou hast shewed unto thy servant; for with my staff I passed over this Jordan; and now I am become two bands," (Gen. 32:10). Paul declares, "I have learned, in whatsoever state I am, therewith to be content," (Phil.

4:11). It is not enough to *hear* duty; Christians must learn *to do it.* They hear it every Lord's Day in preaching, reading, or discussing the Word, yet Paul was a practitioner. Contentment roots in understanding spiritual things, above nature's temporal realm—the "deep things of God," (1 Cor. 2:10), into which angels peer (1 Peter 1:12). Men, naturally dead (Eph. 2:1), cannot learn as corpses, yet God enables them to grasp spiritual mysteries, granting a gracious, Holy Spirit-influenced, contented spirit when they are regenerated, "But godliness with contentment is great gain. For we brought nothing into this world, and it is certain we can carry nothing out. And having food and raiment let us be therewith content," (1 Tim. 6:6-8). One might object, are we not discussing daily bread, not contentment? Yet, can one pray for daily needs without discerning what, how much, or whether they truly need it versus merely wanting it? Such a spirit fosters right prayer. James warns, "Ye ask, and receive not, because ye ask amiss, that ye may consume it upon your lusts," (James 4:3). Christians can pray wrongly or half-heartedly, asking amiss. God answers no unprayed prayers, nor grants beyond what is asked, whether rightly or wrongly. Paul instructs, "Be careful for nothing; but in every thing by prayer and supplication with thanksgiving let your requests be made known unto God," (Phil. 4:6). What if they pray without thanksgiving or begrudgingly? It equates to asking amiss. A proverb stings those chasing wealth or deeming poverty more spiritual, "Remove far from me vanity and lies: give me neither poverty nor riches; feed me with food convenient for me: Lest I be full, and deny thee, and say, Who is the LORD? or lest I be poor, and steal, and take the name of my God in vain," (Prov. 30:8-9). Contentment is divine, implanted by the Spirit, not acquired but infused. Yet, returning to the *petition...*

What is daily bread but life's necessities? Contentment is implied, yet necessities must be met. Cannot one pray *generally* for a week or month? A man might pray over grocery bags to cover a week, fearing to forget. Yet Christ urges daily prayer, not sporadic petitions. Among necessities, bread is most common and vital: "And ye shall serve the LORD your God, and he shall bless thy bread, and thy water; and I will take sickness away from the midst of thee," (Exod. 23:25). God promises provision. In Scripture, bread is prepared for sustenance, a substance appointed for nutrition, not inherent but a divine gift, as the ancient prayer was prayed: "Blessed art thou, O Lord, King of the Universe, that bringeth forth bread from the earth." Ordained to preserve mankind from perishing, it must be used lawfully, enjoyable especially to the hungry: "The full soul loatheth an honeycomb; but to the hungry soul every bitter thing is sweet," (Prov. 27:7). Bread renews strength, preserves life, enables work—without it, men sicken and die. It is universally necessary; rich and poor, presidents and citizens, young and old need it until death. Often the greatest earthly blessing, people sacrifice much for it. None are excluded from gaining it unless oppressed by sin or circumstance, failing to love their neighbor. Bread is essential to common happiness; billions without food render wealth useless. Without *bread*, desperation and violence arise, as seen in inflation's torrents.

The Father is the Giver of life's necessities, freely and graciously providing temporal benefits for His people. Men, cursed, deserve nothing, yet the Father sustains all for their good, granting vocations tied to this petition. Do people think God conjures sustenance magically? A lawful vocation is integral; praying for magical provision without means is foolish. Is not the Father the Possessor of heaven and earth? All men have is His gift: "The earth is the Lord's, and the fulness thereof; the world, and they that dwell therein," (Psalm 24:1). "For every beast of the forest is mine, and the cattle upon a thousand hills," (Psa. 50:10). Men lease from Him, enjoying lawfully, not immoderately—contentment's design. "The silver is mine, and the gold is mine, saith the LORD of hosts," (Hag. 2:8). God ordains all possessions, determining bounds of habitation (Acts 17:26), appointing what each shall have through lawful vocations for His Kingdom's glory—whether in righteousness or justice. Nothing occurs by chance, all ordained for Christ's glory. God grants men a right to use daily necessities lawfully, never sinfully or immoderately. He providentially gives even the wicked cattle and bounty, though they abuse His gifts, their portion confined to this life (Psalm 17:14). God sustains all earthly blessings' continuance: "To uphold all things by the Word of his power," (Heb. 1:3). Without His support, comforts fade; without lawful enjoyment, worse still. The rich and famous, lacking joy, often self-harm despite abundance, missing the blessing's joy.

If God grants anything, He sustains its lawful use. Life and strength enable men to use provisions; otherwise, death renders them inert. He sustains ability to work for bread. Rich, poor, or middling, all may squander gifts through self-destruction, nullifying Kingdom utility. These necessities must be used in a "sanctified use," employing daily bread holily through lawful vocations, received with daily thanksgiving for Kingdom usefulness, desired for all brethren and oneself: "Give us, our daily bread." The Kingdom community is in view, unless one misses the petition's intent, praying selfishly. Those neglecting work or the believers' community miss the mark. Technically, this is a prayer for a capitalistic society, not socialistic—emphasizing lawful effort. Christians acknowledge God's blessings for themselves, their brethren, and all men, that the Father's name be hallowed, His will done, and His Kingdom consummated through the Spirit's influence everywhere. Things are used not only for men's good but for God's glory with thanksgiving for the Kingdom's benefit. Doing good in the Kingdom is active and passive: actively, using good things for Kingdom work; passively, receiving blessings. Giving to a church's ministry or preparing a meal for the sick exemplifies sanctified use of silver, gold, or bread for brethren's good.

Contentment in the temporary, used for the Kingdom's good, is a grand blessing tied directly to this petition. "Give us this day our daily bread" seeks provisions necessary for believers, fostering contentment and quietness of mind in their holy use for themselves and their brethren. Do Christians desire satisfaction and contentment in all things? It is not solely about their own bread. God's promises extend far: "Behold, I will send you corn, and wine, and oil, and ye shall be satisfied therewith," (Joel 2:19). This petition seeks not only God's blessing in necessities but also contentment in what is given daily, for both self and others. The Christian's joy in contentment lies not merely in receiving necessities but in the rightness of mindset toward what God grants: "...a man's life consisteth not in the abundance of the things which he possesseth," (Luke 12:15). What, then, does life consist in? God freely and graciously bestows these good things through constituted means, out of His bounty and goodness—a merciful Giver. The petition reflects the humility of those praying daily, mindful they deserve nothing, indeed the contrary, having forfeited life and comforts in Adam, setting themselves outside God's protection by sin, death, and covenant-breaking: "...and so death passed upon all men, for that all have sinned," (Rom. 5:12). Were it not for God's *grace* in Christ, bread would be the *least* of their troubles, as they provoke God to curse them in coming and going, per the covenant's stipulations. In this way, Christ begins with the beatitudes: "Blessed are the poor in spirit: for theirs is the kingdom of heaven," (Matt. 5:3), for such know their place before the Father, the King of heaven.

This Kingdom prayer, in its fourth petition, urges Christians to ponder its eschatological aspects, considering the consummation of Christ's Kingdom throughout. It is never merely superficial. "Thou shalt not lie" entails living, walking, and upholding truth. This petition—encompassing the Kingdom, Spirit-influence, holiness, and the Father's will for worship—carries end-time implications of Kingdom fulfillment in Christ. His merit brings the Kingdom's fullness, including provisions sustaining the body through lawful vocations until He calls a saint home. Though focused on daily necessities, this petition retains an eschatological element. What should Christians ponder in praying for daily bread and work? Daily bread points to eternal bread that perpetually sustains, with the Christian's mind fixed on something greater.

Christ *is* the Bread of Life. This daily bread carries a spiritual dimension. Scripture portrays a sacred, holy bread on the Table before the Lord in the Tabernacle and Temple: "And thou shalt set upon the table shewbread before me always," (Exod. 25:30). This prefigures Christ. The shewbread, or "bread of faces" in Hebrew, consisted of twelve cakes in two rows, set continually before God's face from Sabbath to Sabbath, symbolizing the faithful multitude presented to God in His church, mediated by Christ, the bread of life: "For as often as ye eat this bread, and drink this cup, ye do shew the Lord's death till he come," (1 Cor. 11:26). Christ Himself is this bread: "I am that bread that came down from heaven," (John 6:50). To those who eat Him by faith, He is to their souls what bread is to their bodies—more essential than bread for physical sustenance—providing spiritual strength, comfort, and refreshment. He is the celestial, spiritual bread, the manna in type: "...satisfied ... with the bread of heaven", (Psa. 105:40).

This spiritual bread—Jesus Christ—is the true bread (John 6:32), the eschatological, Kingdom, sacramental bread (1 Cor. 11:28), the bread of God and life (John 6:33, 35). Prepared by the Father as a fitting Savior—"A body hast thou prepared me"—He perfectly fills the soul receiving Him, bearing mercy, kindness, goodness, gentleness, compassion, and sympathy for His people and sinners He renovates, bringing them into His kingdom. From His fullness, we receive "grace for grace," ministering to the poor, feeding, filling, and satisfying them. Ordained to save His people from mankind, He is "my Salvation to the ends of the Earth." Though perfectly suited as Mediator for souls' good, if not used per the Giver's intent, Christ is misused. Careless men perish this way, like the Prodigal starving apart from his father's house. Christ must be used per God's prescription. To a hungry soul sensible of need, He is pleasant and sweet: "Unto those who believe he is precious." He came "not to call the righteous, but sinners to repentance," (Luke 5:32). Christ renews, strengthens, and preserves souls; without Him, they lack strength and die in sin. When renovated, He makes souls habitable for His presence, fitting them for kingdom business: "Without me ye can do nothing." His Spirit's presence is essential. Universally necessary, He is needed by rich and poor, president and peasant, young and old, until death: "...there is no other name given under heaven, by which men can be saved."

As the bread from heaven, He is the chiefest among ten thousand, altogether lovely. Wise men forsake all for Him—Moses did; David asks, "Whom have I in heaven but thee?"; Paul counts all loss for Him (Phil. 3:8). His sublime virtue must be drawn out by faith: "Except ye eat the flesh of the Son of Man, and drink his blood, ye have no life in you." Free to all, none are barred from this Bread, yet those refusing it perish, losing their souls in hell. Christians must seek, ask, knock, strive, and labor for this imperishable bread (John 6:27).

Christ is essential to holiness and happiness—no joy, peace, contentment, or freedom from depravity without Him: "For he that hath not the Son, hath not Life, but the Wrath of God abideth upon him," (John 3:36). He is the Bread of God—the Light, Joy, and Life of the soul, *satisfying* as God's *life* in men. Earthly bread perishes, but Christ, the living Bread from Heaven, was dead but lives forever, interceding, never dying. Having satisfied the Father's will on the cross, He, as shewbread, mediates between God and sinner, sustaining believers by His Spirit. Unchanging—yesterday, today, forever—He is enduring, refreshing life for the soul, secured eternally for those who have Him. This petition urges Christians to consider this Bread and its daily means of attainment.

Such a petition reveals God's great goodness in providing bread, *both* spiritual and physical. What bread do you need? All things needful for this life. Why daily bread? It encompasses *daily* necessities. God does not desire you to seek yearly bread in a single annual plea; it is your daily necessity to consider these things *daily*, and Christ daily. All acquired through lawful work in God's providence is included in this petition. You ask God to give it: "give us this day..."—acknowledging it as His gift, obtained through His constituted means. The consequence? That you may have contentment with it, blessed by God, satisfying you, fostering contentment, and enabling you to use the strength gained to serve the Kingdom, not the world, flesh, or devil. You seek God to provide all things needful through your lawful vocation, pointing you to the next life, with His blessing therein. Setting your mind, rightly is a grand blessing, as is considering these matters correctly. It manifests Christ's great goodness in promising to be Bread and food for us—an indispensable necessity to pray this prayer, coming to Him to receive His goodness and Himself. It is not merely about eating and drinking: "For the kingdom of God is not meat and drink; but righteousness, and peace, and joy in the Holy Ghost," (Rom. 14:17). Why did Jesus not simply say to pray for the Spirit's Kingdom-influence in daily necessities? He did, implicitly, urging love for our Father collectively, in a heavenly, sublime pattern, to live holily, honoring His name, engaging in Kingdom business through Spirit-influence against darkness, with God providing all needed through lawful vocations, extinguishing fears of tomorrow. This trusts His promises, power, provision, and mediation. All soul-bread, all spiritual life, resides in Him. This shows the blessedness of those partaking of Him: "He that hath the Son hath life; and he that hath not the Son of God hath not life," (1 John 5:12). Temporal necessities yield to the spiritual in this prayer.

God will surely grant temporal things. Thomas Manton observed, "Many say they can trust God for eternal life, but cannot trust him for daily bread."[14] Men, overly enamored with tangible things, pursue them immoderately, deeming them paramount. Without them, they grow discontent, forgetting God gave Christ, ensuring all things for this life and the next (Rom. 8:32). Christ exhorts, "But seek ye first the kingdom of God, and his righteousness; and all these things shall be added unto you. Take therefore no thought for the morrow: for the morrow shall take thought for the things of itself. Sufficient unto the day is the evil thereof," (Matt. 6:33-34). Desiring temporal things is not wrong, but it must be lawful, Christian, Kingdom-oriented, serving the King. Metaphorically, it pains God when His children prioritize corn, wine, and oil over grace, mercy, and the Spirit, as the prophets lament. This petition aligns with "thy will be done"; immoderate desires betray the prior petitions.

Be content with what God provides in your job, family, and life. This does not mean ceasing work, presuming contentment negates effort—illogical, as temporary things perish, and the petition seeks daily bread through daily means. God employs constituted means; your fridge does not magically fill. Be thankful and content for what you have: "in the living God, who giveth us richly all things to enjoy," (1 Tim. 6:17). Does God not prepare a table, as Psalm 23 attests? Consider a

---

[14] Thomas Manton, *The Complete Works of Thomas Manton*, vol. 1 (London: James Nisbet & Co., 1870), 157.

house stripped to studs—electricity, plumbing, all removed—rebuilt over six months' labor. What accomplished it? God's blessings wed to industry: "Except the LORD build the house, they labour in vain that build it," (Psa. 127:1). Seek daily bread through industrious work, asking God's aid. All necessities are sweetened by acknowledging God as Provider, enhancing contentment. When God's kindness goes unnoticed, mercies are not used for His service. His gifts, given in grace, can be bestowed as He wills: "The rich and poor meet together: the LORD is the maker of them all," (Prov. 22:2). Lawful use serves God; misuse or exploitation turns good into sin, missing Christ as heaven's Bread. Most Christians overlook work or Christ as the Bread of Life in this context, prioritizing physical needs over holiness, awaiting magical provision rather than heavenly Bread.

Daily necessities, if unreflective, become snares. Adam and Noah sinned in excess with necessities; such can trap us if not viewed rightly. Never indulge excessive delight in temporal things, diverting minds from Christ, the Bread from Heaven. Manton warns, "Because God stands upon his sovereignty; you must stand to God's allowance, though he gives to others more, and to you less; for God is supreme, and will not be controlled in the disposal of what is his own."[15] You cannot determine

[15] Thomas Manton, *The Complete Works of Thomas Manton*, vol. 1 (London: James Nisbet & Co., 1870), 164.

your portion; Christ reserves that governance. Strive for contentment with your Kingdom allowance, for without it, enjoyment falters.

In this, you depend daily on Christ, your spiritual nourishment, awakening to His Kingdom's heavenly things and end-time fulfillment, toward which all necessities point. Pray thus:

> "Lord, I ascribe to you glory, who is the Heavenly Benefactor, who opens your hand, and fills all things living with plenty. Let it be your good pleasure to give me, and all who wait on your beneficent love, our food in due season in our industry; Give us Bread, and all that is comprehended by it, health, food, raiment, and all the necessaries of life. Give us, O Heavenly Father, daily bread, nothing to gratify our desire for luxury, but such a competence as your Divine wisdom sees fit for us. Give us, O bountiful Creator, daily bread this day, Teach us to live without covetous anxiety for tomorrow, with a trust and dependence on your Fatherly goodness, and to be content and thankful for our present portion, for your love has indulged us. Give us Our Bread, that which is our own bread, by honest labor, and grant that we may never eat the bread of idleness, or of deceit. Give us our bread, for unless you give it, we cannot have it,

> and together with our bread give us your blessing on it, otherwise our bread will not nourish us. Above all, give us the Bread of Life, the Bread that came down from Heaven, the Body and Blood of your most Blessed Son, to feed our souls to eternal life. Blessed Jesus, O that it might be my food, as it was yours, to do the will of your Heavenly Father!"

You are to pray that of the Father's free gift you may receive a competent portion of this life's good things, enjoying His blessing with them.

In the next chapter, we will consider the topic of *forgiveness*.

Chapter 6:
Forgive Us Our Debts

Matthew 6:12, "And forgive us our debts, as we forgive our debtors."

The aorist active imperative of ἀφίημι, "to forgive," carries connotations of "release from" or "pardon," referring to canceling the guilt from failing to follow God's holy law. The term ὀφείλημα, "debt," denotes "sin" or "doing wrong," encompassing transgression and associated guilt in relation to God's law and holiness. It represents the moral debt incurred through sin, used metaphorically as a synonym for sin, with the parallel passage in Luke 11:4 employing ἁμαρτίας, "sins," instead of "debts." Sin is a debt owed to God, any lack of conformity to or transgression of His law. All sins are moral obligations left undone or done wrongly. Christians, obligated to obey God, incur a debt when they fail, needing cancellation since they cannot repay it, knowing the wages of sin is death. "Debt" is a *metaphor* for sin.

The contrast, "...as also we have forgiven our debtors," implies that just as Christians forgive others, they seek God's forgiveness. Yet, this is not a debtor's ethic where their forgiving compels God to forgive them. Having forgiven those who offended or sinned against them, the implication is significant but must be rightly understood. It is not that forgiving others causes or merits God's forgiveness, nor does Jesus suggest forgiveness to the degree they forgive others. Rather, the force lies in the manner of forgiveness: forgive us as we forgive others, suggesting Christians live upholding the first three petitions. Forgiving others does not earn forgiveness but reflects a renewed disposition making forgiveness possible. A connection exists between being forgiven and willingness to forgive, even if done weakly. The privilege of receiving forgiveness entails, the responsibility to forgive others. Faith does not merit salvation but must be present to receive it; likewise, a forgiving nature does not merit forgiveness but must be present, evidencing a heart poor, meek, and pliable. An unforgiving person cannot receive forgiveness, unable to pray for what they do not know. Stubborn or begrudging hearts, unyielding to the Spirit, cannot work forgiveness in themselves or others, lacking the qualities of peacemakers or the poor in spirit. Without an intimate relationship with the Father, forgiveness—received or given—is impossible.

Doctrine: God's forgiving is the motive to our forgiving, for Christians pray that God would forgive them of their sins, being daily reminded that they are indebted to God.

The pardon gained in justification by the Father's declaration, on Christ's behalf, applies to all sins—past, present, and future. When declared just, God removes all guilt and penalty by declaration. Justification is not experienced directly but through its fruits, as the Father's declaration, based on Christ's covering, is external to believers: "For by one offering he hath perfected for ever them that are sanctified," (Heb. 10:14). Believers must believe this, trusting God's promises. Justification is not repeated; no one can charge the justified elect with condemnation, as they are established in Christ as heirs of eternal life, co-heirs with Christ of all the Father prepared before the world's foundation. Yet believers continue to sin post-justification, necessitating daily prayer for forgiveness of debts incurred: "For in many things we offend all," (James 3:2). Some claim conversion erases their sinner status entirely, denying they can be called *sinners* due to justification. Yet, "If we say that we have no sin, we deceive ourselves, and the truth is not in us," (1 John 1:8). Such libertines deceive themselves, excusing sin or self-flattering; justified Christians are not wicked sinners under condemnation but remain debtors, sinning still. As Luther made famous and said, *simul justus et peccator*—at once just and sinner.

Christ taught daily prayer for forgiveness (Matt. 6:12), and saints historically sought daily pardon: "I acknowledged my sin unto thee, and mine iniquity have I not hid. I said, I will confess my transgressions unto the LORD; and thou forgavest the iniquity of my sin," (Psa.

32:5). Antinomians, bolstering grace, claim believers' sins apply only to the old man, negating the need for forgiveness. Such are heretics, oversimplifying a complex truth. How is one justified, forgiven, yet seeking forgiveness? In justification, believers are declared just by faith alone, blood-bought by the Savior, their hearts regenerated by the Spirit, longing to follow Jesus in His ways and commandments. Yet the old man, that rotting corpse, persists. The Father removes sins penalty but not the *sense* of daily sin's guilt, which produces separation, sorrow, and repentance. Believers are burdened to confess daily sins, conscious of grieving the Spirit: "How then can I do this great wickedness, and sin against God?" (Gen. 39:9). Joseph, though not guilty, knew the shame sin would bring. Christians seek daily assurance of forgiveness for any sin, resting on promises like, "And if any man sin, we have an advocate with the Father, Jesus Christ the righteous," (1 John 2:1).

Confession and prayer for forgiveness are *daily* necessities. Christ taught disciples, without exception, to pray for forgiveness. John affirms, "If we confess our sins, He is faithful and righteous to forgive us our sins, and to cleanse us from all unrighteousness," (1 John 1:9). Daniel prayed thus: "O Lord, according to all thy righteousness, I beseech thee, let thine anger and thy fury be turned away from thy city Jerusalem, thy holy mountain: because for our sins, and for the iniquities of our fathers, Jerusalem and thy people are become a reproach to all that are about us," (Dan. 9:16). Daily, believers acknowledge the high and lofty Father, worship Him, regard His name as holy, seek Kingdom influence by the Spirit, strive to keep His will by His Word, request provision, and confess sins. Daily confession aligns with the prayer's *daily nature* across all petitions.

There is a need for the removal of corrupting wickedness in the Christian's life. In dealing with both forgiveness of sins and the need to be kept from temptation, both of these confront sin directly. Both revolve around the removal of sin—a destruction of sin, a mortification of it. Both have been addressed in walking in newness of life, within the first three petitions before the Father. It is noteworthy that forgiveness is not first but fifth. How is sin to be removed in the life of a believer who is justified and yet still, day by day, sanctified and more conformed into the image of Christ?

Sin in the life of a believer is taken away either by the forgiveness of sin that has been committed or in which one lacks conformity to the law, or by protection against it so that the believer does not commit it. The Christian knows full well that they and all others in the church are guilty both of original and actual sin, and by it become debtors to the justice of God. They know that neither they nor any other creature can make the least satisfaction for that debt they all owe to God. You see "our sins"—they are very aware that all the members of Christ are in the same boat. They pray for themselves and others (consider the words "*our* sins"), that God of His free grace would, through the obedience and satisfaction of Christ, apprehended and applied by faith, acquit them both from the guilt and punishment of sin, and accept them in His Beloved Christ, daily. This is to be a daily thought. Acquittal is a means to further holiness, so it is a *daily* thought. And not only that they are accepted, but that they continue in His favor and grace, with pardon for their daily sins, filling them with peace and joy, in giving them daily, more and more assurance of forgiveness. They are emboldened to ask and encouraged to expect it because it is directly attached to Kingdom-influence, Spirit-influence in the furtherance coming of the Kingdom. And when they have the truth of that testimony in their heart, not only do they experience it themselves, but from the heart they too forgive others their offenses. They are not justified daily, but they recall in the petition their justification daily and look for a sense of forgiveness each day in all their wayward walking for sanctification.

The *forgiveness of debts* is a metaphor. The reason for the metaphor is because by God's law and His immutable justice, Christians are bound to God, to give Him their entire obedience. Any point of departure from His revealed will in any degree of this obedience, falls under the penalty of the covenant and the curse of the covenant, or they would have, had it not been for Jesus Christ interceding on their behalf. They ought to think about whether they are exemplifying life or death, justification or not, sanctification or not, Spirit-influence or not. Such sins are called debts by Christ, because they lack, any and all obedience which they owed to God. And they carry with them, as all the commands do by way of curse, an obligation to undergo those punishments associated with them. They are reminded about what they owe daily.

Forgiveness is pursued and requested by the believer for these debts, whether in want of conformity to or transgression of the law of God. God removes the hindrance of sin by grace and blessing, in Christ, where the wonders of Jesus are obtained; He is, in fact, the wonder of wonders; to gain the forgiveness of sins from an infinite God is a wonder. And so, He gives His people all good things that they lack or desire for their good. The forgiveness of sins committed after justification, that tend to the well-being of the holiness of the believer, that they might better exercise all their duties before God in compliance to Him, depends on the well-being of a very necessary and essential part of being in union with God through Christ, which is really the sum of the first three petitions.

Is not sin a great wickedness, and would it not be better to suffer the greatest affliction than commit the least sin? They are the heaviest of all evils. Jesus knew all

His disciples understood the idea of being indebted to another. How much more terrible is it and heavy is it to be indebted to the God of the universe who cannot be appeased but perfectly? They are taught to pray for the removal of sin in an absolute manner, to be forgiven of daily offenses, with a disposition that they forgive others, and to be kept from all offenses, to be kept from all evil. Christ assumes Christians will have daily offenses. What a sad thought that is from the Savior who thought and knew, in light of the very cross He was going to, that Christians would have a daily need to rely on the Father's forgiving nature. Daily they need to pray for sustenance. Daily they need to pray for forgiveness. Every part of their life and communion is a walking, step by step, a light for every step by His Word, because sin spoils everything daily, minute by minute, second by second. Sin is the great spoiler of communion with God. Though a believer is in union with Christ and God, sin spoils communion. Sin gives birth to all kinds of great miseries in this life and it hinders the sanctifying influence of the Spirit, especially when the believer grieves the Spirit in their sin.

Sin brings the Christian into a face-to-face confrontation with daily sins that stir up the reminder that they are indebted to God, and that they would be continually indebted to Him, further and further were it not for Christ. Sins are called debts, and daily debts need to be confessed and forgiven daily for sanctification to increase. God's law has bound all sinners to suffer for their sins, if they cannot satisfy God for them. What will they do to appease the wrath and curse of God in the covenant? They know they cannot remove such a debt, and they will never be able to satisfy the Father's dissatisfaction. Rebels, criminals, sinning against God's holy character, and nothing they can ever do can wipe away the stain and filth of sin. And the believer, in knowing this, has such a stirring within himself, that he knows that such is true, and he cannot pay any debt, especially to God, for *sin*. They have a perpetual threatening condemnation in their own consciences as Joseph did to commit wickedness. How can I do this great wickedness and so sin against, not Potiphar, or his wife, but God, first and foremost. Sin would have hindered his communion with God.

The believer knows that only by the mercy of God in Christ can any of his debts be forgiven, by way of metaphor. He is, to pray daily for His *sanctifying* spiritual influence, kingdom influence, on him in this way. Is it merely to mouth the words in this way that give him satisfaction—some people think so when they repeat the Lord's Prayer. They think reciting the confession of the words alone grants forgiveness. But they have misunderstood what it means to be conformed to Christ further and made more holy and so they misunderstand daily repentance, which is what Christ is pointing the disciples to. They are to run to the forgiving mercy of

God every day, and do so with a heart for God. They are not merely to mouth the words as the papists do. He is their Father, is He not? He is their forgiving Father as much as He is a providing Father, and a holy Father, and a heavenly Father. What will they be reminded of and how will they pray for pardon of sin in their daily walk? Will they merely say, "forgive us our debts," and leave it at that? And believers know that the Father's mercy in Jesus Christ is of an infinite nature that only the work of Christ enables Him to forgive sin, no matter how heinous their sins might be. They know they come to the Father daily for forgiveness. And that is not the same as repenting. Christians often confuse the two. They ask to be pardoned without ever intending to repent of that which they are asking for pardon, things they have done, and so they pray to appease their conscience asking nonetheless, which makes their asking amiss because they do not understand the kind of heart and disposition they are to have when they ask, which is to have a forgiving nature. Jesus covered that disposition in the beatitudes. Such a petition is daily, because they must daily remember all these things because they are forgetful people because evil makes them forget or become confused, and it disrupts their communing with God.

The Christian is to daily remember that all men, considered in the state of sin and alienation from God, are in captivity. Men, under the curse of the fall, are "captives," and "bound in prison," and the work of Jesus Christ as Mediator is to "bring out the prisoners from the prison, and them that sit in darkness," (Isa. 42:7). Men are in the dungeon of the curse of God, and are debtors and will not come out until they have paid the last penny; how long will they remain there? They are described in Scripture as "captives," Isa. 59:25, "Thus saith the Lord, even the captives of the mighty shall be taken away, and the prey of the terrible shall be delivered." Such people, due to the fall, due to the subtlety of the angelic serpent called the great Dragon, the devil, they are in captivity as prey to Satan. How will they be delivered? They cannot be delivered unless they pay the debt they owe for being both fallen and all the actual sins they commit, as a result of being fallen as criminals and rebels to the Father. Christians take that so glibly as if they just have to say, "forgive me" and all is well. Christ said, "The Spirit of the Lord GOD is upon me; because the LORD hath anointed me to preach good tidings unto the meek; he hath sent me to bind up the brokenhearted, to proclaim liberty to the captives, and the opening of the prison to them that are bound; To proclaim the acceptable year of the LORD, and the day of vengeance of our God; to comfort all that mourn; To appoint unto them that mourn in Zion, to give unto them beauty for ashes, the oil of joy for mourning, the garment of praise for the spirit of heaviness; that they might be called trees of righteousness, the planting of the LORD, that he might be glorified," (Isa. 61:1-3); these people are very broken, and need a spiritual physician. There were in bondage, and Christ releases His people from captivity. They are given liberty and everlasting life in Him; and become Kingdom people, Spirit-influenced people. What does Christ do but deliver by way of paying the debt owed. The wages of sin is death. As a debt, God is the creditor and He will be paid, and all who do not pay will instead pay the eternal price for every sin they have ever thought, said or done. That is why hell is forever. Christ teaches His disciples to be reminded of His everlasting covenant and work, and how forgiveness of the debt of sin to God is paid by an eternal price; and that, to consider it daily; and, to act in accordance with it daily; otherwise their petition about holiness and Spirit-influence will not occur.

Debts, sins, make men accountable to God to be put into an eternal prison for non-payment. With sin, non-payers go to hell, as Christ says, Matt. 5:25-26, "Agree with thine adversary quickly, whiles thou art in the way with him; lest at any time the adversary deliver thee to the judge, and the judge deliver thee to the officer, and thou be cast into prison. Verily I say unto thee. Thou shalt by no means come out thence, till thou hast paid the uttermost farthing." How long is that? Because of the curse of God on the fall of men, they are prisoners for sin. They are bound in the prison-house because they have wasted the goods of their Master, and contracted a debt that they are no way able to pay; and if it is not paid for them by someone who is able, there they must stay forever. In Adam, *all* mankind was cast into hell's prison for that great debt. Such is the place of rebels and criminals.

When men transgress against God, who is the Judge of all their actions, their disobedience commissions a debt, and such disobedience is sin and its wages is death. The Father is the creditor to whom these debts are due. This is why in Matthew 6:12 Jesus explicitly has His disciples praying daily for forgiveness as it applies to their holiness, to the Father, "Our Father which art in heaven, ... forgive us our debts." It is to the Father that men are indebted with such a debt. Pardon carries with it an experience of liberty. Imagine the Christian life as one with no emotional requital of liberty. To not feel as though one is forgiven? It would be an intellectual striving after thinking through justification without any recourse to being comforted in sanctification if that were the case. Would that not be hard? It would be devastatingly hard to live under the guise of justification without sanctifying Spirit-influence and pardon. To know one is forgiven without ever feeling as though the guilt is ever taken away is a terrible thought; many Christians live this way.

Now this notion of being forgiven as one justified, one time, with the entirety of the spiritual blessing, is a counterpart to that which is experienced by disciples of Christ daily—they go together; for justification and sanctification are inseparable. That is why nominal Christians have such a very hard time with this. To claim *justification*, one must show *sanctification*, or the justification which they claim is *counterfeit*. The reminder is set in the Christian's mind, that daily they are to petition the Father to keep them in a state of remembrance (daily) to what Christ has done, and continue in a humble attitude because remaining sin is constant, and to experience sanctification by remembering their justification. If they have faith, if they have a changed heart, they are in this state of desiring applied forgiveness and a constant conforming and sensibleness in their prayer. Not that they think they have to be justified again and again. There are many people in the church today at large which think as a papist thinks, as if a sin can be bigger than the work of the Savior, and cancel out the infused goodness that Christ has implanted by the Spirit in the soul, and so they have to work to gain back that which they lose in justification. What a *horrid* doctrine that is. They fall in and out of grace every day; and if that notion is held to, and one can fall away from the work of Christ, then Christ is no Savior; and they can never have assurance of eternal life. The libertines are of the opposite idea, that since Christ did what He did, no other recourse of any kind is necessary. But Jesus told them to pray about this daily. The disposition of the Christian is one that recalls time and time again what Christ has done, and yet, still needs further humility, a growing degree of its affect in them. This is why forgiving others, in like manner, comes into view.

Are these Christians merciful? Are they like the Father who forgives them? By mercy Christians are ready to console and assist those found in any misery, just as God is. By patience and longsuffering, they are inclined to bear much with an offender (Matt. 17:17), to forgive offenses, no matter how serious (Matt. 18:21-22), just as God does. It is the manner in which God forgives criminals against His holy character; is rebellion by the sons of Adam and the daughters of Eve, heinous in God's sight? How offended is God? And yet He is forgiving. Pick any sin, pick any commandment and run through the branches of wickedness attached to it in between the believer and the Father; what does it mean to lie, and not hold to the truth, and take that commandment and run its course as to how the Christian repeatedly does not live up to all their expectations as God so orders them in truth telling and truth contending and the propagation of the Gospel in every area of their life. How is God wronged by them in it? Will the believer in this consider that God ought to be ashamed to be called his God for such great wickedness? They are at *war* with sin, yet, *when* they sin, they are not *so much* at war with it. What they want to do, they do not do, and what they hate, this they keep on doing, *though* God hates it too. But

God is forgiving and longsuffering because of Christ; but is that the whole story?

What will the Christian think of this as it relates to those that abuse them, in not such an evil way as they in fact abuse their own heavenly Father? God daily forgives the penitent. By kindness, in which they conduct themselves even with the greatest offenders against them and even so, heap benefits on such enemies, allowing the course of godliness to rule their whole life, even in the midst of the hardest providences with others. As the Father forgives them their great indebtedness and daily indebtedness in sins, do they forgive others? Justification gives way to holiness, which gives way to action. The practical dimension of this is both toward God and others. To have one is to have the other. Not that one earns the other, but that they are alike. Just as the Father does for them so they have hearts to do for others, even though they may be ill-used. However men ill-use the Christian, the Christian then has those people as debtors to them, for not upholding the commands to love them as a neighbor. What is the Christian to do? Should he retaliate? They are abused by others by unjust violence. They are abused in their vocations at work. They are abused by not giving them what is their due, wages, raises, equipment for work and such like things. They are defrauded in their possessions as by thieves. They are in reputation and in their good name taken and abused. What ought a Christian to do? Forgive them because God is more abused by the Christian who has been forgiven. There are certainly consequences for sin; as a thief is to be jailed for thievery. But forgive them. As slanderers may be jailed or fined for slander. But forgive them. As those unlovely, do not love as they ought, still, forgive them. It does not gloss over the commands, it just places them in the perspective they need to be in because they are reminded that they abuse the Father daily.

Forgive others when they are abusive in all those ways, because it shows the Christian's disposition and heart as one which is forgiven as a criminal and rebel themselves against God. Does not God permit and ordain any and all abuses the Christian suffers? And what do trials procure but an opportunity for being more like Christ and being more holy? What will they do?

What is this *petition* getting at? Sensible prayer is where this petition leads; *sensitivity*. It is here that Christ teaches believers to pray for the sense of pardon, and the manifestation of this sense to their own souls. Without which it will be a hard Christian road to walk. Such prayer suits believers very well, though all their sins, past, present, and to come, are already pardoned before the Lord as it pertains to being justified. Luke 6:37, "Forgive, and ye shall be forgiven," take note of the manner, and the action and see that their forgiveness is required as previous to God's forgiveness of those daily sins because they are not to have a revengeful spirit.

They must be practical in their walk and not just Christians who talk about following the Lord. When they lay down their sins before the altar of God and offer Christ for them, God will forgive them if they have a forgiving spirit. In other words, a Spirit-changed heart will yield them a forgiving Father. Christ teaches in the parable of the king and the servants, Matt. 18, that the king forgave the servant, and the servant must do likewise, and he calls him back when he doesn't because the servant shows he was not a loyal subject of the king, "I forgave thee all that debt, shouldst thou not also have had compassion on thy fellow-servant?" "We seek this remission as a benefit we yet lack, but speak of our remission as a duty we in the present do."[16] Or as Edwards says, "Col. 3:13, "Forbearing one another, and forgiving one another, if any man have a quarrel against any: even as Christ forgave you, so also do ye"; and in the next verse but one, "And let the peace of God rule in your hearts." We cannot make one prayer that is acceptable to God without this, Matt. 6:12. God has told us he will not otherwise forgive us, Luke 11:14–15. We can never expect to maintain peace with men, except we do in this way."[17] God's forgiving is the *motive* to our forgiving.

---

[16] Thomas Boston, The Whole Works of Thomas Boston: Sermons and Discourses on Several Important Subjects in Divinity, ed. Samuel M'Millan, vol. 6 (Aberdeen: George and Robert King, 1849), 71.

[17] Jonathan Edwards, "Living Peaceably One with Another," in Jonathan Edwards Sermons, ed. Kenneth P. Minkema (New Haven,

How many times have Christians mouthed this prayer in ignorance, rattling off the words like a rote incantation, blind to the fathomless depths that lie beneath them? Does it not plunge into the very marrow of the soul, this plea for forgiveness, a chasm so vast that to skim its surface is to miss the divine drama unfolding within? They just repeat it, these unwitting pilgrims, without ever pausing to let its weight settle upon their hearts, as if reciting a grocery list to the Almighty rather than crying out from the dungeon of their depravity. But do we truly rest in this petition, leaning upon it like a weary traveler upon a staff, remembering with all our heart's fervor that we fly to the Father's mercy, nestling into its embrace and building our hope upon its unyielding rock? Are we roused in the blaze of our justification to contemplate the slow, stubborn forge of our sanctification, where sins are not merely pardoned but pursued to their graves?

You cannot earnestly beseech the blotting out of your sins unless you first confess them with a shudder, hate them with a holy fire, and detest them in yourself and in the world around you, as one recoils from a serpent coiled in the cradle. Repentance marches hand in hand with such a cry, an inseparable companion in this pilgrimage of pardon; what profit is there in begging forgiveness while clutching the very daggers that

---

CT: The Jonathan Edwards Center at Yale University, 1723–1724), Rom. 12:18.

pierced the Father's heart? What a hard, halting Christian life awaits the one who petitions for mercy but refuses the *metanoia* that mercy demands—no repentance, no genuine alteration of the soul's compass; no turning from the slough, no ascent toward holiness. Forgiveness without change is an oxymoron, a contradiction as absurd as a river flowing backward or a sun that sets in the east; it mocks the very grace it claims. "Forgive me, Lord," the hypocrite whispers, "but I intend to wallow in this mire regardless"—and what is that, pray tell, if not the growl of a heart still chained to the flesh? Is that the disposition etched in the Beatitudes, those luminous signposts of the kingdom, or merely the mutter of a prodigal who has tasted the fatted calf but spurned the robe?

You might venture, with a wry twist of logic, that we ought to have traversed the Beatitudes before venturing into this prayer, laying the foundation stones before raising the walls. To a certain extent, yes—they stand as the *preamble*, the preparatory thunder to this petition's lightning. Poor in spirit, those who mourn, the meek who inherit the earth, the merciful who taste mercy in return: these are the hues that color the canvas of true supplication. But it is no great riddle to grasp that one cannot rightly magnify the mercy of God—the very refuge to which the soul flees—without first being refashioned to receive its balm, suited like a beggar reclothed for the banquet, that the remission of sins might not scald but soothe.

Nor can you presume upon the mercy of God without mirroring the Father's own disposition toward sin, extending mercy as freely as it has been poured upon you; to clutch grace like a miser's coin while withholding it from your neighbor betrays no change of heart, no pulse of the new creation. Mercy and love toward our brethren serve as the echo, the outward ripple, of the mercy and love God has lavished upon us. "As we forgive our debtors," the prayer itself insists, weaving this reciprocity into its warp and woof. Mercy and love are not hoarded treasures but rivers shed abroad in our hearts by Christ through the Spirit, and those in whom they flow cannot but let them overflow in turn, forgiving all injuries and wrongs inflicted by others as freely as the dawn scatters dew. God forgives you without price or precondition, and He yearns for you to mirror that prodigality, extending grace as the fruit of grace received. Yet mark this well: God does not overlook sin, turning neither a blind eye nor a indulgent wink; He exacts its full penalty, laying it upon the shoulders of Jesus Christ in that shadowed hour on Calvary. Even so, He desires you to emulate this pattern—not in the punishing, but in the pardoning: from His special, sovereign mercy toward you flows the call to be gracious in kind, the effect rippling through your life like light through stained glass. God's forgiving is the grand motive to our own, the fire that kindles our fumbling flames.

Has a thief pilfered from your storehouse? Report him to the watchmen of the law, by all means, and yet forgive him from the depths, as the Father has forgiven your pilferings from His infinite store. Has a slanderer besmirched your name before the assembly? Set the record straight with quiet firmness, and forgive him nonetheless, letting the venom drain harmless into the dust. Did not Christ Himself declare, just verses prior in that Sermon on the Mount, "Blessed are the merciful, for they shall obtain mercy," (Matthew 5:7)? He did not proclaim blessedness upon those who triumph in theological jousts, out-arguing their rivals with sharpened quills, nor upon the revengeful spirit nursing its grudges like a dragon its hoard. No, the stamp of justification, that divine seal upon the soul, impresses itself in merciful deeds; it stands as evidence, a title deed we may scrutinize in our quieter hours, assuring us of the Lord's mercy because we have tasted and extended mercy in our turn. And herein lies the rub, the gritty test of its authenticity: do we live in accord with this grace, or does our conduct *belie* our creed?

Christ is not merely bidding us look to God for daily forgiveness, as we do for bread or breath in this petition's broader sweep; He is summoning us to walk in its train, to journey with steps more holy, more worthy of the mercy that woos us onward. Do you seek forgiveness, then you must tread the path of the forgiver, for the two are as intertwined as vines upon an arbor.

When you harbor hatred toward another, a bitter root burrowing deep, you cannot offer any sacrifice acceptable to God, as the altar itself recoils from such defilement (Romans 12). Hear Christ's own words, "Therefore if thou bring thy gift to the altar, and there rememberest that thy brother hath ought against thee, leave there thy gift before the altar, and go thy way; first be reconciled to thy brother, and then come and offer thy gift," (Matthew 5:23–24). Oh, and observe how He loops it back: "Forgive us our debts, as we forgive our debtors." Otherwise, you cannot approach the God of love with hatred festering in your bosom, in any of its cunning disguises—be it grudge or grudge's subtler kin. When you draw near with such a warped heart, it impairs the very channel of access to your heavenly Father, like a dam across a stream. Even husbands and wives, whom Peter presumes to tangle in the ordinary frictions of the wedded state, are exhorted to weigh their bonds with hearty consideration, lest one nurse anger toward the other; and what is the peril he names? "That your prayers be not hindered," (1 Peter 3:7). Sin, in its many guises, can throttle prayer, withholding good gifts not from spite but from the Father's wise restraint. What holds true for husbands avails for wives as well, and for sons and daughters, brothers and sisters, the whole household of faith—they are "heirs together of the grace of life," (1 Peter 3:7), knit as one in Christ Jesus. To withhold honor, especially from the weaker vessels among us, erects a barrier to prayer, for it grieves the Holy Spirit and dishonors alike, the Father's love and the Savior's redeeming grace.

If mere disagreement can in this way impede prayer—*choking* the kingdom's power through the Spirit's influence in our relations—what devastation does a lack of love wreak, or a refusal to forgive? What ruin does a revengeful spirit unleash, that serpent uncoiling in the soul? Until you purge this terrible attitude, root and branch, you will find your course corrupted, your Christian practice stumbling like a lame horse over uneven ground. As John warns, "But he that hateth his brother is in darkness, and walketh in darkness, and knoweth not whither he goeth, because that darkness hath blinded his eyes," (1 John 2:11). You will tumble more readily into sin and error, confounding your path, mistaking the very essence of forgiveness, and lacking the heart to walk its demanding way. And make no mistake: you will not grow, stunted as a tree in barren soil, your branches barren of fruit while the orchard flourishes around you.

Lastly, consider the *daily rhythm* of this petition, as constant and necessary as the pulse in your veins. Just as we plead for daily bread—sustenance to carry us through each fleeting day—so too must we daily seek pardon, nestled as this request is in the heart of the prayer, inseparably bound to the hallowing of the Father's name, the coming of His kingdom, and the doing of His will. Could you dare approach these weighty matters without first addressing the God whose name is holy, whose will is sovereign, whose kingdom reigns eternal? As you ask for bread to nourish your body, so you must daily beg for forgiveness to cleanse your soul and grace to steel you against temptation's wiles—daily, daily, daily, a ceaseless cadence of dependence. Under the old covenant, the law prescribed a lamb offered every morning and every evening, a daily sacrifice ascending to God (Numbers 28:4–6). So too must you daily look to the slain Lamb, the Christ, following Him whithersoever He leads, pressing near to Him, abiding in His presence, as a child clings to a father's hand.

This daily petition for forgiveness is *not* an afterthought but a necessity, even for those already justified, already pardoned through the blood of the Lamb. To come before the Father daily, seeking the remission of sins, is to drink deeply from the well of sanctifying grace. Though you are changed—adopted into God's family, justified by faith in Christ Jesus, and made heirs of eternal life—you still walk through a world thick with the mist of sin, like travelers in Peru where rain never falls but a clinging dampness dirties every street, every building, every surface. Imagine trudging barefoot through such a city, the grime of the day caking your soles; without cleansing, you'd carry that filth always. So it is with your soul, daily you contract the contamination of sin, the subtle accretions of a fallen world, and daily you must come before the Father, washing your conscience in His mercy, partaking anew of the benefit of His pardon. And as you are forgiven, so you are called to forgive others, mirroring the grace that has cleansed you.

So, pray this way:

> O Lord, for the sake of Your infinite mercy and the merits of Your beloved Son, forgive me and all penitent sinners our debts—our sins, whether known or hidden, of omission or commission, those vast liabilities we owe to Your righteous justice. Forgive us, O Lord, as we forgive all who are indebted to us, even our bitterest enemies, whose wrongs against us are but a trifle compared to the towering debt we owe You. We give You glory, O Lord, who teaches us love, who has made our forgiveness a mirror of the grace we are to reflect in our lives toward others. What a gracious condition of pardon! Who would cling to a grudge, refusing to forgive a brother a few pennies in this fleeting life, when ten thousand talents are forgiven for eternity in the next? O Lord, let our love learn from Your love to us—not only to forgive our enemies but to be zealous in

doing them good, as You have done to us in boundless measure. For God's forgiving is the motive to our own, a daily reminder to Christians that we are debtors to grace, ever bound to reflect the mercy we have received.

Chapter 7: Lead Us Not into Temptation

The Lord's Prayer now turns to a shadowed frontier, where the soul pleads in Matthew 6:13, "And lead us not into temptation." This petition, far from a casual aside, plunges into the perilous realm of temptations and testing. The verse cries, "do not lead us into temptation, or a time of testing," with the Greek εἰσφέρω—an aorist active subjunctive meaning to "cause to, to bring in to, to lead to." It speaks of bringing or leading someone into a particular state, here denoted by πειρασμός, the condition of being tempted, tested, or enduring a time of trial. The phrase μὴ εἰσενέγκῃς ἡμᾶς, "lead us not," carries the weight of an imperative, a desperate entreaty: "Don't let this happen!" It signifies being subject to, or kept from, a certain state, acknowledging God's sovereign hand over every path trodden. This πειρασμός encompasses temptation to sin, trials, afflictions, and the sinister enticements of Satan, the Evil One. Though God does not tempt to sin, He permits His disciples to be tested and tried in His providence, not as the active tempter but as the One who orders all circumstances. Christ instructs His followers to pray for deliverance from such testing, recognizing their frailty and propensity to sin.

In this way, the petition implores God not to allow His disciples to enter any state exposing them to temptation's snare, lest they fall into sin, or, if faced with it, to be kept from succumbing. Such testing recalls Job's crucible, where faithfulness is laid bare, whether in the face of simple sin or the dire precipice of apostasy.

The *doctrine* distilled from this text is resolute: Christians are to pray daily to navigate faithfully through trials, afflictions, and temptations, without being overwhelmed by immoderate responses to them.

This sixth petition, though twofold in expression, forms a single plea, here addressing its first half: a negative request that the Christian not be led into temptation. It is a cry to avert disaster, to shield the soul from succumbing to the flesh's weakness in the daily traverse of a fallen world. It seeks God's grace to forestall an unhappy outcome, that believers might not be tempted at all; or, if temptation arises within God's sovereign purpose, that they would not yield to its pull. Should they stumble into sin, when temptation overtakes and prevention fails, the prayer is that they not be wholly consumed but rescued from the lion's maw or the bear's paw. Whether this is one petition or two is of little consequence; more likely, as Christ binds both clauses—"Lead us not into temptation, and deliver us from evil"—into a single truth, they form one supplication with two facets. The first seeks preventing grace to keep Christians from falling into evil; the second seeks recovering grace, that even if they fall, they are not utterly cast down, for "the LORD upholdeth him with his hand," (Psalm 37:24).

This prayer against temptation acknowledges that all times are in God's hands, subject to His sovereign disposal as King. Christ may order His people's lives as He deems fit, His prerogative as sovereign, always for their good, though the path may be strewn with thorns. The believer's weakness, stained by sin, prompts a plea to this King to order their lives so they are not battered by the world's abuse beyond endurance. The world is a cruel adversary—why court its blows? God's omnipotence could halt any trial or temptation at a whisper, and so His people, wholly dependent, implore Him to spare them from such ordeals. No one, in sober reflection, pines for a Job-like trial, muttering, "I wish I had the humility of Job"—a prayer as daunting as it is rare. Who would choose the fiery furnace, the lions' den, or forty days in the wilderness, tempted by the devil himself? In this petition, disciples glorify God's authority and power, marveling at the breadth of His reign and the might of His administration, which daily shields them from temptation's dominion. By His strength, as Paul declares, they are powerful and strong (1 Corinthians 16:13), fortified in the power of Christ (Ephesians 6:10), echoing the apostle's cry, "I can do all things through Christ who strengthens me," (Philippians 4:13).

Temptations are no strangers but *common* evils, prowling since the fall, pressing the faithful to veer from the straight path into crooked ways. Therefore, this petition, like its fellows, is framed for daily use—day by day. Temptation takes center stage, where wicked motions entice God's people to sin, whether through the corruption of their nature, the world's allurements, or the devil's schemes. To tempt is to test one's faith, patience, and love toward God, a sifting procedure where subtle suggestions threaten to shake true grace from the heart, leaving only corruption's dregs. God does not tempt directly but places Christians in times of pressure, refining them as diamonds; Satan, the malicious one, wields temptation for harm, not God. Such sin springs from one's own desires, as James 1:14 warns, "And every man is tempted when he is drawn aside of his own concupiscence." Lust is the tempter, though the event may be ordered by God's providence. It is a trial of God's power and justice, testing whether He can and will help or harm. As Exodus 17:2 questions, "Wherefore do ye tempt the Lord?"—men tempt God through distrust, failing in trials, as if under probation to reveal whether their profession matches their heart. When one falls to temptation, overcome by weakness, they yields to wicked motions, drawn into the orbit of the world, flesh, or devil, relying ever more on God for deliverance—they end up being in a fearsome place of standing.

Christ, as Hebrews 2:18 assures, "being tempted he is able to succour them that are tempted." Tempted in body and soul, yet *without* sin—tested by God in His passion and agony (Luke 22:44), by the devil in the wilderness (Matthew 4:1), and by the devil's minions throughout His earthly life—He knows the weight of temptation. Clothed in human nature, He understands pain, the toll of temptation on heart, mind, and soul, and comforts His people in their distress. He became man to pity men, a merciful High Priest to all.

Men face trials in this arena from God, their own hearts, the world, or the devil. God tests, as in Genesis 22:1, when He commanded Abraham to take his only son, probing through prosperity or affliction to reveal what lies within—good or bad, as Deuteronomy 8:2 recounts: "And thou shalt remember all the way which the LORD thy God led thee these forty years in the wilderness, to humble thee, and to prove thee, to know what was in thine heart, whether thou wouldest keep his commandments, or no." Does God not know? Of course He does, but He tests to show His people what they possess or lack, that they might rely on Him and seek what is wanting. How does God "tempt" without sin, unlike the world, flesh, or devil? By trying what is in them—grace or sin, real or counterfeit, Ruth's fidelity or Orpah's retreat. Sometimes He delays help to test where they turn, how swiftly they yield or seek Him, how they wield the Spirit's sword against sin, or whether their resolve falters. Afflictions, as 1 Peter 1:6 notes, bring manifold temptations to try faith. Christ tests not only what grace they hold but how much of the old man lingers—dead, dying, or still shackling them with original sin's daily weight. Sometimes God grants abundance to see what they do with plenty, or withholds to test where they seek fullness. What will David do in the wilderness, pursued by Saul, his heart breaking over a cut robe? What will David do on the rooftop, passions aflame, descending to bloodshed with Uriah and immorality with Bathsheba? The David of the cave and the David of the rooftop reveal how trials, in varied circumstances, lay bare the heart's disposition.

To such an ordinance of trials, God declares in Jeremiah 6:21, "Behold, I will lay stumbling-blocks before this people, and the Fathers, and the sons, together shall fall upon them." How terrible that sounds, a metaphor of stumbling blocks crashing down upon them. If Christians seek out or search for sin, God will open the door to those places and even give them over to it for a time, setting traps from which they must be rescued. Will they walk through that door or not? In distressing times, when Christians feel as though God is not with them, He may also withhold grace. Consider Hezekiah, in that most famous passage every Christian should heed, "God left him, to try him, that he might know all that was in his heart," (2 Chronicles 32:31). What a harsh reality Scripture reveals about God's dealings with His people. It is a serious plight to confront sin in such extreme ways, that Christians might see what they lack, what they need, and how strong they are. They must pray daily for strength, for Kingdom influence, for resistance to all temptations—half of which they might not even see clearly. It is needful sometimes that Christians should see how they are able to perform before God in the Spirit, or not; it helps to answer the question, "Am I a good Christian?"

Such a time of temptation is never for God's information. God does not order life to discover what is in men's hearts; He knows this already. As John 2:25 states, "And needed not that any should testify of man: for he knew what was in man." Psalm 139:2 echoes, "Thou knowest my downsitting and mine uprising, thou understandest my thought afar off." This essential wisdom of God, where Christ is called in Proverbs 8:1 and Matthew 11:19, holds all the treasures of wisdom and knowledge (Colossians 2:3), and is named the wisdom and power of God (1 Corinthians 1:24). He shows the *right application of all His knowledge*, using it wisely for His people, for His glory, not to find out what is in the heart, but to show His people to themselves and to others what is truly there. Are they like Orpah, or are they like Ruth? Trials are most informing at this point; Orpah and Ruth should know in themselves what they are, for generally, Christians tend to desire the lowest amount of service to God with the highest rewards they can gain from Him.

Consider also the trials, afflictions, and temptations that arise from the heart and from the world. Christians have hearts renewed, yet still carry the remnants of remaining sin. Before conversion, their hearts were desperately wicked in every way and thought, as Jeremiah 17:9–10 declares: "The heart is deceitful above all things, and desperately wicked: who can know it? I the LORD search the heart, I try the reins, even to give every man according to his ways, and according to the fruit of his doings." In man's unregenerate heart is nothing but the depravity of blackness. From such original blackness come all actual sins, any want of conformity to or transgression of God's Law, what God says. Pick any sin, and it dwells in the heart; if not for the grace of God, it would remain there, stirred up in all kinds of wickedness, so that there is nothing new under the sun as it pertains to evil. The Christian is fully aware of his tendency to sin, carrying the old man of sin even after the Spirit's influence grants a new heart. When they choose sin over pleasing God, all manner of evil is dredged up and spills out. The devil, to be considered in the second half of this petition, did not make them do it. They did it, chose it, and are immoderate in whichever way they turn in trials, afflictions, or temptations to give in. Christians are not internally compelled to sin by anything but their own lusts; they are always sinners by their own choice. Is Satan's hand on it? Yes, his hands are on all sins, even by extension, for he is an *original liar* and *murderer* of souls; all sins stem from his temptation in the garden, of envy (consider the way the commandments are structured to end with that sin). But he has only as much power as a Christian grants him. James 1:14 reminds, "Every man is tempted, when he is drawn away of his own lust, and enticed," to sin. For Christians, the remnants of remaining naughtiness in their hearts suffice to sin most heinously. Pick any sin, the most heinous, and the Christian remains liable to commit it.

Being a Christian does not exempt them from grievous sin. The flesh stirs them to sin, or at least tries to. Paul laments in Romans 7:15, "For that which I do I allow not: for what I would, that do I not; but what I hate, that do I." What a powerful active principle presses the Christian immoderately to sin against the blood of Christ. The old man is always admonishing and pressing them to sin. As the word of God is living and active in the Christian soul, so is sin, stemming from the corruption of the corpse they carry in their heart. It is dead, but not gone, still exerting effects. Take any dead corpse, lay it on your couch, and you will quickly see its effect, though dead. Leave it there, and one cannot help but smell or see its influence when passing through the room, an interchange though it is dead. They pray daily to deal with it moderately and submissively, that they would not be led into temptation beyond what they can handle.

The world works in conjunction with what the old man once desired, and the toxic character of that old nature *still* stinks, anointing the Christian's thoughts negatively, rendering them as a head in the clouds, bumbling without heed to their actions. Where can they go, to what can they turn day in and day out, but to *watch and pray*? The world surrounds them, their flesh accompanies them, so what can they do? The more they are influenced by the world, and the more their flesh is swayed by it, the more time the world has over them, the more they are conditioned in unexpected ways. What part of the world has *immoderately* pressed in during just the past week? Can a Christian be unconcerned without self-observation? Trials, afflictions, and temptations are birthed by giving into these, carried away by hearts that desire them. What will take them from sitting under the Apple Tree with great delight? Are they praying daily to be protected from all hindrances, to have power to face any encounter? Yet, in all of it, there is a goodness. Not that trials, afflictions, and temptations are good—they are not—but they are to count such things as joy, as James exhorts.

Christ's leading this way, though His people pray for deliverance, is always part of what is good. A Christian might think, "I'm thoroughly confused; are temptations good things? Are we not to pray against being led into them?" Christ brings His people into Job-like testing either in mercy or judgment. How strong is their grace, how resolved their mind? Or how weak are they in using the word, failing to walk straight in this short distance, from here to there? Will they make it without incident, or be immoderate? When hell's mouth yawns on one side and a quagmire on the other, will they fall in? Christ reveals His people's flaws, and as hard as it is, it is for their good. Why? "For our profit," that "we might be partakers of his holiness" (Hebrews 12:10). Thomas Manton, in his work on the Lord's Prayer, noted, "When we say, Lead us not into Temptation, we do not beg a total exemption from God's trials, but only a removal of the judgment of them."[18] This is particularly insightful. To be exempt from temptation or trial is to be removed from the world, from God's providential governance post-fall. A "total exemption" is to be in heaven; to pray against God's good governance? This petition does not pray that no trial, affliction, or temptation ever touch them—that is impossible in this life. Christians live in a sinful world, where Christ promises tribulation. All trials, afflictions, and temptations are necessary for refinement in holy living, without which one would not grow holier. What would they fight against? What would they strive for? How

[18] Thomas Manton, The Complete Works of Thomas Manton, vol. 10 (London: James Nisbet & Co., 1872), 394.

would they walk? Would they merely presume salvation?

Consider 1 Corinthians 10:13: "There hath no temptation taken you but such as is common to man: but God is faithful, who will not suffer you to be tempted above that ye are able; but will with the temptation also make a way to escape, that ye may be able to bear it." The petition asks that trials, afflictions, or temptations not be immoderate beyond their ability to bear. No *thinking* Christian prays, "Lord, I want no trials, afflictions, or temptations ever again." That would overrule Scripture's teaching, the book of Job, 1 Corinthians 10, and Christ's own life, including God's covenant of redemption with its suffering servant. Many Christians mistakenly think this petition means nothing should ever touch them. Rather, it prays that trials, temptations, and afflictions not be too hard, that they not become immoderate in them.

How does one navigate Christ's *school of affliction* without offending Him? To offend is to pray for the removal of all temptations without considering what He has ordained, turning prayer into sin by desiring God to alter His providential order, as if they know better. Christ prayed, "O my Father, if it be possible, let this cup pass from me: nevertheless not as I will, but as thou wilt," (Matthew 26:39). If they must pass through the fire, so be it, as God wills. Many Christians shun this prayer, twisting it into, "Do not allow any trial, affliction, or temptation near me." The true petition is, "Do not give me anything too hard, and help me not be immoderate in thought, word, or deed. Grant the grace to accomplish Your will. Keep trials and temptations as far as possible, but not my will but Thine be done, for Your glory and my good in holiness." In trials, Christians should beware of murmuring against God rather than fulfilling His will, praying wrongly for instant deliverance without Spirit-led growth or further instruction.

When the trials, afflictions, and temptations come, *how* will the Christian *submit* in them to God? Certainly, they are not looking to invite them, for all those difficulties they are looking to avoid if they can. "My brethren, count it all joy when ye fall into divers temptations," (James 1:2). James is not teaching that Christians ought to run into wickedness, so that they might be able to quote Paul and say, where sin occurs, grace abounds all the more, how great is that! Paul doesn't mean that. He knows what sin is and what it does and how lust in original and actual sin ruins everything. Rather, James says when Christians fall into trials, afflictions, temptations, count it all joy. It is to have a moderate view of God's providence and government. These are not to be that which the Christian desires; that would make them a masochist. A masochist is a depraved individual who obtains pleasure from receiving punishment. No *Christian* desires affliction. Trials, afflictions, and temptations are not to be desired, but rather used in a sanctifying manner when they come. They are *harnessed for holiness*; that would be a better thought.

The petition in the prayer then changes radically from, Lord stop evil of any kind from touching me, to: Lord, help me moderate all trials, afflictions, and temptation that you ordain for my good as they come that I might be strong in your power and in your grace. Frailty and fragility are seen in such things, they uncover what is frail and fragile, and in need of strengthening or corrections, so that Christians see what they lack or need. Grace is sought, Spirit-influence is sought. Link all of the petitions together to see it in this one. *Heavenly Father, help me to be holy, that you may be glorified, that my life would stretch into eternity as a straight way along a fine line by the Spirit-influencing power of Christ, that day to day I would trust you, and continue to do so, even when all trials, afflictions, and temptations come my way that I would not be immoderate, but be steadfast for your glory and your kingdom according to your will. Wow*, the Christian thinks, *that is a helpful way to pray; I'd not thought of it that way.*

No one ought ever to pray this petition thinking that God will keep all tribulation from them. It's promised they will have tribulation. "In the world ye shall have tribulation," (John 16:33). They are to, as he directed, "watch and pray." Why are they to watch?

Should they not just pray if this petition means keep all evil of every kind and every instance away from me? They are to be engaged in battle against the world, the flesh, and the devil, and there is no chance, if they are Christians, that those three will leave them be. Are they ignorant of that fact? Are they then not provided for against all trials, afflictions, and temptations to do the will of the Father? Are they not armed with the Spirit-influence of the word they are to wield and are they ready to do battle? How will Christians be moderate in trials, afflictions, and tribulations if they think they must merely pray their way out with no work to be done? Sensible prayer is done by the truth, and without the truth they cannot pray, without the word they cannot pray. What effective means will they engage in this? How will they wield the weapons of their warfare in war against the world, the flesh, and devil? Will they merely mouth the words, "lead us not into temptation?" Are they to be "praying always," of course, that is the channel of the Spirit's influence to heaven. But is that all? What spiritual habits will they use in the fight? Think about all the people, all over the world, who merely mouth the words, without ever understanding Christ's *intent*? What will they do without God's power and Christ's power and the Spirit's power wielded as a responsible weapon?

I think Christians need to wed better the promises of the word with the work of prayer; to bring them together as weapons better. Here is a promise to the church, "Because thou hast kept the word of my patience, I also will keep thee from the hour of temptation, which shall come upon all the world, to try them that dwell upon the earth," (Revelation 3:10). Jesus does promise some temptations they are kept from for the faithful in certain circumstances. He does not say all, but the promise is that he is most assuredly aware. And he will do them good. "The Lord knoweth how to deliver the godly out of temptations," (2 Peter 2:9). He doesn't say he will in every instance, but he knows. And they in such a knowledge, are to daily pray about dealing faithfully in all trials, afflictions, and temptations, without being immoderate in them. It is the substance of the first part of the petition.

Are you sometimes overwhelmed living in the fallen world? One of the most difficult times of being immoderate in trials, afflictions, and temptation is being overwhelmed and giving up in a duty. You might think, "This Christian life is no bed of roses, and it is too hard, and I am so weak." When discouragement occurs, you fall into all kinds of temptations. Maybe you even give in so easily, and wonder, time and time again, why didn't I do so and so when that sin raised its ugly head? Why didn't I first act this way when that tribulation came? Why didn't I watch and pray the way I know I should have and yet, I gave in? Or, how about this one, "I didn't even consider that such and such was a sin at all." You have to know, first, that nothing happens by accident. You cannot be tempted without God's will. And yet, you cannot resist the difficulties associated with trials, afflictions, and temptations, without the power of Christ working in you by the Spirit on your behalf.

Let's assume for a moment that everything you are doing, you are doing well. As it pertains to your job, or your schooling or your homemaking or your devotions or your walking in a straight line, you find, you are walking on a very well laid direct course. Let's assume it. Yet, you wonder why things are not so well with school, or your job or your devotions, or that such spiritual sensibility in prayer seems to be discernably lacking. Things seem a little cold, and you think, to no fault of your own. You know, first of all, that nothing ever happens to you without God's will first ordaining it. I've written at length in other places, extensively, on the providence of God. He orders all kinds of things for you for your good, and yet you do not think that trials and afflictions and temptations are good. Did Jesus think being led into the wilderness by the Spirit in Matthew 4:1 was good? To be led into the wilderness of the world in trials and afflictions and temptations is hard.

You will need to make a distinction in Jesus' intention in this petition, as it also pertains to the disciples. It has some specific connotation in it, for it deals with being faithful, as a disciple, and in their particular sending out to preach, that they would not encounter opposition that they could not handle, or that would lead them astray, so astray as to apostatize. Eleven made it to the end, one hung himself. God's allowance of trials, afflictions, and temptations in refining holiness is one thing, but to lead into temptation is often a work of judgment. God may allow you to be tempted, as the Sovereign God of the universe, allowing trials, afflictions, and temptations for your good, but to be *led* in that direction? What does that mean? It is akin to the idea of a giving over, of a sort, as Paul uses in Romans. Which is a very scary prospect. But as it concerns Christians, he may allow it, but sometimes he leads them into it, and sometimes that is harshly. He may bring you into trials, afflictions, and temptations, that you will be battered and mistreated by the world, the flesh, or the devil—see Job.

Here is the way the *1647 Westminster Confession* uses certain Scriptures in this, in which we often either neglect, or we use to excuse ourselves in 17:3. "They may, through the temptations of Satan and of the world, the prevalency of corruption remaining in them, and the neglect of the means of their preservation, fall into grievous sins; and for a time continue therein: whereby they incur God's displeasure, and grieve his Holy Spirit; come to be deprived of some measure of their graces and comforts; have their hearts hardened, and their consciences wounded; hurt and scandalize others, and bring temporal judgments upon themselves." For Christians after holiness, that is a *scary* proposition. Most want to exempt themselves from that paragraph. But as much as God gives the trial, so there is also the way out for you. Christ, knowing how to comfort you, he alone can give strength to resist and overcome whatever crooked ways you must avoid.

God will give you grace to fight, and fight well, and pray well and be moderate in your walk. When Joseph was assaulted by Potiphar's wife, the Spirit gave him a motivation, a thought, that is inscribed for all time, "How can I do this wickedness, and sin against God?" (Genesis 39:9). The motions and movings of the Spirit aid you in overcoming the trial, affliction, or temptation. When Jesus was assaulted, what did he use, but the word of God, "It is written, it is written, it is written," (Matthew 4:4, 6, 7). Where shall your help in any of these things come from, but the Lord? "I will lift up mine eyes unto the hills, from whence cometh my help. My help cometh from the LORD, which made heaven and earth. He will not suffer thy foot to be moved: he that keepeth thee will not slumber. Behold, he that keepeth Israel shall neither slumber nor sleep. The LORD is thy keeper: the LORD is thy shade upon thy right hand," (Psalm 121:1–5). It is vital to go to God, to Christ, for he skips upon the mountain and leaps upon the hills to your aid. He will dispense grace and will aid you if you trust in him. How do you go to him? What will he give you if you do not daily come to him for what you need? Daily holiness, daily bread, daily forgiveness, daily deliverance? Do you go boldly to his throne and mercy seat, and touch the top of his golden scepter? Are you searching for the end or aim of this petition which is a confident humility in submission to the Great King?

Pray this way:

> O Lord God, you see how our enemies, the world, the flesh, and the devil, are every moment soliciting, enticing, alluring, or tempting us to evil. O be merciful to us, save and help, and deliver us. You see how weak I am, and how ready my own deceitful heart is to surrender itself to trials, afflictions, and temptations. O lead me not, if it is your good pleasure, to fall into violent or lasting temptations, that may endanger my perseverance. I know, O heavenly Father, that to be tempted is not sin, for your own Son, God incarnate, was tempted to the most horrid of all sins, to fall down and worship the very devil. And yet I know sin lies in yielding to temptation. If you as a trial of my love, lead me into any great temptation, and let me continue under it your will, Lord, be done, not mine. Let your all-sufficient grace restrain my consent and keep me always on guard, watching and praying, and let me at last be more than a conqueror. I am

content, if it is your will, to enter into trials, and afflictions, and temptations, for your glory and my good. Christians are to daily pray about dealing faithfully in all trials, afflictions, and temptations, without being immoderate in them.

In the next chapter, we will look at the second half of the verse, to consider *deliverance* from the Evil One.

Chapter 8: Deliver Us from the Evil One

The Lord's Prayer now reaches its final plea in Matthew 6:13, "but deliver us from evil." The *Didache* (c. 140), of unknown authorship, intertwines Jewish ethics with Christian liturgical practice to form a whole discourse on the "way of life." It exerted an enormous amount of influence in the patristic period and was especially used in the training of those coming into membership in the church.[19] It renders the petition, "And do not lead us into temptation, but deliver us from the evil one."[20] Cyril noted, "'Lead us not into temptation,'" as Luke concludes the prayer, but Matthew adds, "but deliver us from the evil one." There is a certain close connection in the clauses, because when people are not being led into temptation, they are also delivered from the evil one. "If anyone were perhaps to say that not being led into is the same as being delivered from it, he would not err from the truth."[21] But there is more to it than that.

---

[19] Ancient Christian Commentary on Scripture: Introduction and Biographic Information (Downers Grove, IL: InterVarsity Press, 2005), 491.

[20] Joel C. Elowsky, ed., John 11–21, Ancient Christian Commentary on Scripture (Downers Grove, IL: InterVarsity Press, 2007), 250

[21] Arthur A. Just, ed., Luke, Ancient Christian Commentary on Scripture (Downers Grove, IL: InterVarsity Press, 2005), 189.

The words carry precise weight. The conjunction ἀλλά, meaning "but," signals an emphatic contrast, a pivot from the previous plea. The verb ῥύομαι, an aorist middle imperative, means to deliver or rescue, with the intent of preserving, implying rescue from severe and sharp danger. The term πονηρός can mean anything evil or wicked, but also "the evil one." Why can it go either way? The Greek phrase τοῦ πονηροῦ, "the evil," may be translated as things that are evil or as the evil one, referring to moral corruption or the devil himself, who personifies evil as the one who is essentially evil. Jesus uses this phrase in His prayer to keep His people safe: "I pray not that thou shouldest take them out of the world, but that thou shouldest keep them from the evil," (John 17:15). Paul echoes this, saying, "But the Lord is faithful, who shall stablish you, and keep you from evil," or the evil one (2 Thessalonians 3:3). The petition assumes some testing and temptation from the former request *will occur*. The first clause is positive, "lead us not into temptation," while the second is negative, "but deliver us from evil," or the evil one. Keep us from entering into testing, but if it is necessary, rescue your people from it.

What is meant by "deliver us from τοῦ πονηροῦ *the evil* or *Evil One*"? Evil is just that, evil of all kinds—any spiritual or temporal affliction or evil pertaining to the fall. As it refers to the devil, Satan desires to use any opportunity to his advantage, so if testing of any kind ought to come about in the Christian's walk, this is a petition to be delivered from the Evil One and his purposes in such a time. It is a plea for preservation during times of testing, as if one is praying, "If it is your will do not permit us, since we are weak by nature and prone to sin, to enter into situations which in the natural course of events would expose us to temptation and cause us to perform terribly and fall, but, whatever is your providential way with us, deliver us from the evil one."

The *doctrine* is clear: Christians pray not to be kept under the power of the devil and delivered from the times of trial that evil brings. Trials are brought on by God's providential hand, as are all manner of temptations within those providences, and God often leads His children into these, always for their good. "So now it was not you that sent me hither, but God: and he hath made me a father to Pharaoh, and lord of all his house, and a ruler throughout all the land of Egypt," (Genesis 45:8; cf. Genesis 50:20). "The LORD hath made all things for himself: yea, even the wicked for the day of evil," (Proverbs 16:4). "O Assyrian, the rod of mine anger, and the staff in their hand is mine indignation," (Isaiah 10:5). "For of a truth against thy holy child Jesus, whom thou hast anointed, both Herod, and Pontius Pilate, with the Gentiles, and the people of Israel, were gathered together, for to do whatsoever thy hand and thy counsel determined before to be done," (Acts 4:27–28). Though they enter into temptations and trials, they are to pray against it, with submission to God's will, because, simply considered, it is an evil. It is a petition to not be led into difficult circumstances that set Job-like trials to start. "Blessed is the man that endureth temptation: for when he is tried, he shall receive the crown of life, which the Lord hath promised to them that love him," (James 1:12). "In brief, being conscious of our own weakness, we ask to be defended by God's protection, that we may have an impregnable position against all devices of Satan."[22] Job was plagued by Satan, by God's invitation: "Have you considered my servant Job?" A righteous man, severely tested by Satan with God's permission. Satan's name means "the accuser," and in the book of Job, the reader sees him at work, accusing with all kinds of moral evil. Jesus warns Peter, "Satan wants to sift you like wheat, but I have prayed for you that your faith might not fail," (Luke 22:31–32). It is interesting to note that Jesus does not tell Peter that there will be *no* time of testing. Peter pledges loyalty even unto death, but falls asleep in the garden. Jesus then awakens Peter and tells him to watch and pray lest he enter into temptation. What does Peter do after that? Is he found praying? Soon thereafter, he fails in his time of trial by denying Jesus three times. When Christians pray in their sensible prayer, they are protected by Jesus' cross and

[22] John Calvin, A Harmony of the Gospels, Matthew, Mark and Luke, trans. A. W. Morrison (Grand Rapids: Eerdmans, 1972), 1:212.

resurrection power from Satan and his attacks. Satan the accuser is not prevented from his work as "the accuser," but the disciples are instructed not only to pray in general but to pray for deliverance from the times of trial that evil brings. Then, as much as trials and temptations in this light make life a time of testing, what happens next but that the believer is brought, metaphorically, into Satan's courtroom to be accused.

What is that which is evil? Afflictions and dangers, whatever losses and harms are providentially sent from God, fall under this banner. "Shall a trumpet be blown in the city, and the people not be afraid? shall there be evil in a city, and the LORD hath not done it?" (Amos 3:6). "I form the light, and create darkness: I make peace, and create evil: I the LORD do all these things," (Isaiah 45:7), here translated as great distress. They may be injuries and wrongs done to Christians from other men, those that reward evil for good: "Whoso rewardeth evil for good, evil shall not depart from his house," (Proverbs 17:13). Evil encompasses sin and all manner of evil: "The evil which I hate, that I do," (Romans 7:15). "Woe unto them that call evil good, and good evil; that put darkness for light, and light for darkness; that put bitter for sweet, and sweet for bitter!" (Isaiah 5:20). It includes anything sinful: "If ye then, being evil, know how to give good gifts unto your children, how much more shall your Father which is in heaven give good things to them that ask him?" (Matthew 7:11). It stems from a corrupt conscience or wicked custom: "But let your communication be, Yea, yea; Nay, nay: for whatsoever is more than these cometh of evil," (Matthew 5:37). Satan, by his evil height, is called the Evil One, the Prince of evil who coaxes and tempts to all things opposed to God's goodness and Christ's holy excellency. "And he shewed me Joshua the high priest standing before the angel of the LORD, and Satan standing at his right hand to resist him," (Zechariah 3:1), the great accuser who accuses God's people of their sinfulness. This may also, fitting well into the petition, be taken for the cause of evil, its course, and its evil effects (Genesis 3:5), surrounding the corruption of nature (Romans 7:5), that which is contrary to good (Psalm 37:27), to any well-doing (Isaiah 1:16), trial (Job 1–2), hurt (Genesis 50:15), damage or mischief (Proverbs 17:13; 1 Peter 3:9), danger (Proverbs 22:3), disgrace (2 Samuel 13:16), destruction (Esther 8:6), that which is unprofitable (Isaiah 7:15), things that are troublesome and perplexing (Exodus 5:19). Evil can be applied to angels, all spirits, or men, with relation to their imaginations, communications, actions, and such things.

And what of the evil *one*? The devil, or Satan, is called *the evil one*, for he is in his own nature corrupt and most evil, being the head and captain of all evil beings (both devils and men) and the accuser and furtherer of evil purposes and works (John 17:15; Matthew 5:37, 6:13,

19; 1 John 2:13). The devil is evil in *nature* or *quality*. He was not created this way from God, but by a voluntary departure from God and goodness. He is the origin of evil perfectly, but not infinitely. He will be evil into all eternity, but was not evil from all eternity. When men act like him, what might be said of him is said of men, they act morally evil against the law of God. If the Christian walks a road turned here or there by God's providential appointment, they pray not to be brought into Satan's nearness, not to be led into temptation. And yet, if they are brought near, they ask to be rescued and delivered from his wiles. They are weak, and by nature they are not very good at repelling his attacks, and the fiery darts of the devil are difficult to deal with; things they must endure in battle.

If the petition revolves around the evil one, or Satan, it shows that if God decides, for the Christian's trial and further humiliation, to allow them to be tempted by the devil, they desire, ought to desire, that the devil may not have his will done to them, that they would not be kept under his power. The devil is the evil one, for he is the original sinner, he sins from the beginning (1 John 3:8). He is the greatest sinner, called by the apostle "Spiritual Wickedness" in Ephesians 6:12. His sins are in the highest degree against God in every way and manner, against the Light, with *unreserved* malice and spite against God and all his people. Jesus says he is the father of sin (John 8:44). All the sins of the whole world are because of him, and his original sin in himself, for without the devil, and his fall, there would be no furtherance of sin, neither original nor actual, in the garden. So, he is described as the original sinner, the evil one. Satan is the grand artificer in temptation and all things contrary to the Law of God. He is the one who advances men to sin, being called in Matthew 4 the Tempter. He tempts to endanger the inward man, not merely things men think are evil. Poverty is an evil. Sickness is an evil. He will certainly use these, but he will use all things. Satan will make men rich and healthy, to hurt their inward soul, and have them damned, by being patiently subtle in prosperity. Sin hinders communion with Christ, hinders salvation, and hinders God drawing close to men and men drawing close to God. Afflictions touch that which is temporary, but moral sin and moral evil touch that which is eternal. This is why they are to pray against evil of all kinds, for the origin of evil, that which results from giving into temptations, whether they arise from the world, the flesh, or the devil, are to be prayed against. Watch and pray, lest ye enter into temptation.

Christ has set forth a petition in this, "deliver us from evil or the evil one." This is how Christ prayed, "I pray not that thou shouldst take them out of the world, but that thou shouldst keep them from the evil," (John 17:15). How then should the Christian pray this petition? With a sensibleness of danger. All the petitions set themselves against sensible prayer. Not only to have a sense of what they press the Christian to do as those who serve Christ in his Kingdom, but with a hearty earnestness about how they pray such things with sensitivity to them. They are not praying that their pool pump not break, so to speak. They are praying in respect of everything which may be deemed evil and that might arise as from the Job-like interference of the devil himself. The devil has nothing but malice for the Christian, and his design and desire is to perform that which is evil to press the Christian to choose that which is evil always. He is so effective in this that the state of unconverted men is said to be under his power. "...he also himself [CHRIST] likewise took part of the same; that through death he might destroy him that had the power of death, that is, the devil," (Hebrews 2:14). The devil has the power of death, which is the power of sin, which is the power of evil. "Ye are of your father the devil, and the lusts of your father ye will do," (John 8:44). This is what natural men do because they are *filial* with the devil. He is their father. All those who live in sin, are unconverted, Satan is their father and they are part of his dominion and empire. Satan's kingdom reigns in the heart of men, and they do not even know it. The *accuser* brings men into his courtroom into his dominion, and accuses them to God as being wicked sinners, men of his like caliber and rank. He is not wrong about them, "He that committeth sin is of the devil; for the devil sinneth from the beginning," (1 John 3:8). All natural men are under the power of the devil. They are his children, "O thou child of the devil," (Acts 13:10). They are his subjects, for he rules their hearts by sin. If God does not intervene, and rescue these natural men from the devil and the power of sin, they go to hell and spend their eternity with the devil with his and their family in his place, "Depart from me, ye cursed, into everlasting fire, prepared for the devil and his angels," (Matthew 25:41).

When the devil accuses a Christian of sin, he is often not wrong, but stating the obvious, and yet, God intervenes and will not tolerate slanderous accusations against his people because they are re-robed in new garments of salvation.

The more willingly Christians sin, the more they place themselves under the *devil's* sway, often giving him leave to do his worst. Do they not, then, have a great urgency to pray, "Lead us not into temptation and deliver us from the evil one?" One might think that God is on their side, and He is, and Christ is on their side, and He is, so what can the devil do? The devil, as an artificer of temptation, with his cunning wiles, tries anything to increase the destruction of God's kingdom. He is so bold as to tempt Christ himself, saying, "Since you are the Son of God," (Matthew 4:3). He knew Christ was the God-man, yet tempted Him nonetheless. His malice and anger are so great an evil that he would come against God, thinking he could get the best of Him, or, knowing he couldn't, still continued to show forth the kind of unrelenting evil he is, though a defeated foe. He cannot get the best of God's people, but he will try nonetheless—it is his nature.

Will anyone say they have no need to pray daily, "Deliver us from evil"? They often, wrongly, pray this first, dismissing the other petitions that should be central in their thoughts. Do Christians believe they are so delivered from Satan's power and so brought into Christ's kingdom that they are completely free from the devil's wiles as they traverse this world? Will they walk in a straight line, or prowl side to side, here and there, to be caught by Satan's snares?

How hard is it, really, for the devil to press the Christian's buttons? They have the world's influence, set on course by wickedness and spiritual principalities and powers in heavenly places. They have their flesh to contend with, and Satan uses every tool to take them off course and bring them under his bondage. He will fan the flame of their lusts and corruptions, for, as 1 Corinthians 7:5 notes, the lack of self-control is *offensive* in Christians. Paul said he would not have known what lust is, the lack of self-control, but by God's law. Satan will press one's lusts to boil, to vex and capture them in some trap, to draw them to some particular act of sin to dishonor God. He will do so to place the Christian in a state of disturbance rather than the peace they should have by abiding in God's commands. He will press them to be complacent, to murmur, to distrust God when they walk into a time of testing and trial. Do they not have need to pray, "deliver us from the evil one"? He will press them to abandon holiness, misuse the means of grace, become lax, or, conversely, be immoderately sorrowful about worldly things, to rise in passions and fleshly lusts, to harbor spiritual pride, or partake in unbelief. "Put on the whole armour of God, that ye may be able to stand against the wiles of the devil," (Ephesians 6:11). He has fiery darts that must be extinguished: "taking the shield of faith, wherewith ye shall be able to quench all the fiery darts of the wicked," (Ephesians 6:16). They still carry, *though* redeemed, the old stinking corpse of sin, and the devil tries his best to awaken it.

Even though Satan cannot impose his tyrannical power as lord over their hearts, for they have been delivered by Christ, he tries to revive their lusts and desires in that old corpse and make them resurrect it. He will not yield in assaulting, troubling, and striving against them. They have need to pray, "deliver us from evil." They need God's protection and Christ's Spirit working mightily to pull down such strongholds. Christ tells them, "Call upon me in the day of trouble; I will deliver thee", (Psalm 50:15). How are they to do this? "Deliver us from the evil one." And that daily. Is the Christian not to pray for the hedge of protection about them? It is the same to watch and pray this prayer, so that even the devil takes notice of the strength of prayer about the Christian. "Hast not thou made an hedge about him, and about his house, and about all that he hath on every side?" (Job 1:10). These were the devil's words about Job once God brought up the holy character of that patriarch. How will the Christian be caught unaware of Satan's wiles? It is simply to be ignorant of the devices used against them. Sadly, because of the fall, the Christian must take time to learn these devices. They would much rather think about the sweetness of Christ, delight in Him, and commune with Him, and such. They often have no desire to set forth a war-like strategy against Job-like temptations of the devil. And yet, what will they do if unaware of his devices, for they are constantly in the heart of battle?

Thomas Manton explained it this way, "Would Peter have ever made a motion for Satan, if he had seen his hand? O no; the temptation was disguised to him, when he persuaded his Master from suffering. He covers his foul designs with plausible pretenses."[23] "Then Peter took him, and began to rebuke him, saying, Be it far from thee, Lord: this shall not be unto thee. But he turned, and said unto Peter, Get thee behind me, Satan: thou art an offence unto me: for thou savourest not the things that be of God, but those that be of men," (Matthew 16:22–23). *Let not these things be; be it far from you, Lord: this shall not be to you.* Jesus called him a devil, for the apostle's speech

[23] Thomas Manton, *A Practical Exposition of the Lord's Prayer* (London: J.D., 1684), 485.

was of the devil; it was the same. How much of a Christian's speech is of the devil because they are ignorant of his devices? Christians, often, do not know what they are saying, or of what Spirit they are, even if pressed by the devil. Did Peter? Christians think, no matter what they do or say, or how they serve God, that so long as they act with their best intentions, they are acting of the Spirit, with zeal for God, but it could be of the devil. Do they not have need to go to Christ and pray, "Lord, deliver us from evil"? They have no ability to deliver themselves from anything, which is why they pray daily this way. Can they stand and fight? Not without Christ. They need his covering, as Manton not far after says, they need "his Covenant-strength, that we may be strong in the power of his might, to conflict with Satan."

The devil also uses the tool of the world to afflict the Christian. What did Christ do? He overcomes the one with the power of death, that is the devil, due to the fall, and so reverses the fall. Does He do anything to the world for His people? "Who gave himself for our sins, that he might deliver us from this present evil world, according to the will of God and our Father", (Galatians 1:4). Christians need to be delivered from this present evil world. They are to be transformed by the renewing of their mind, to not have the mind set on things of the world (Colossians 3:1–2) but rather set on Christ. They are constantly barraged by the world because Satan constantly uses the world and stirs up their flesh against them. The world becomes a burden and is immoderately used. Christ becomes replaced by things of the world, even bit by bit. The world and its things become more important and more of a delight than the Lord's Day, or communion, or hearing the preached word; something replaces it because the world is tangible. Prayer makes all things around the Christian sensible, experienced by godly sense, and so they do not want to be insensible to holy things. They want their mind and heart set on Christ, to favor holy things over the world. The world is not an entity itself as if it knocks at the Christian's heart as something with *being*. But the devil uses the tool of the world in its fallen state in that way, and so does the flesh. Do Christians have a need to pray "deliver us from evil"? Daily and constantly?

And then what of the flesh? It is a tool at the devil's disposal and the world's disposal, for it entices the Christian by drawing away the heart towards worldly things. It is a tool used by the devil to cause the Christian to fall into sin and wickedness that it delights in. But it is a tool that, if there were no devil to tempt or world to draw away, would do the job by itself to draw the Christian away from Christ. So, they must pray daily to be *delivered* from evil.

What does that mean as it applies to the *self*? That God would mortify the corruption that is a stinking corpse. Paul said, "O wretched man that I am, who shall deliver me from the body of this death?" (Romans 7:24). Is it not a great mercy from God to be empowered and kept from sin? Sin is a great power indeed, for it took the death of the Son of God and his crimson flow to overcome it. If a Christian falls into sin, what a wonderful promise they have to be delivered from the wilderness of their off-course wandering from under the paw of the bear and mouth of the lion. "And if any man sin, we have an advocate with the Father, Jesus Christ the righteous," (1 John 2:1). They do not desire to wallow in it, like pigs in the mud.

When there is no violence by the Christian in a particular area of sin, no thought about it, to work against it, no desire to break the power of sin from off them, they are giving into sin, and will set themselves under it for a time, and it may even be a heinous sin. Sin still remains in that rotting corpse of the old man in their flesh and, though it does not reign over them, sin still persists, even when there is a great war against it. There is a great tool against it, if it will be but prayed: "Deliver us from evil." It is a praying, watching, striving, waiting, and depending on God for strength.

Such can be prayed because, *annexed* to the prayer is the *promise*. What is the promise in this petition? It is a petition, but what does God promise to do in Christ within it? The promise is annexed to it in other Scriptures: "The Lord is faithful, who shall stablish you, and keep you from evil," (2 Thessalonians 3:3). Pray it, and He will do it—not like a magic prayer, but attached to the ordinances which *cultivate* victory. What is prayer without reading? What is reading without understanding? What are ordinances used wrongly or not at all? What is the armor of God hanging in a closet somewhere? Those who are serious, watchful, careful to get sin mortified when it rears its ugly head, when the devil's wiles are at work, when the world begins to entice and draw away, so do Christians have need to consider all this?

Christ is the Strong Tower to which Christians *run*, and running is given for *praying*; is it a wonder why Proverbs says to run to the strong tower? "The name of the LORD is a strong tower: the righteous runneth into it, and is safe," (Proverbs 18:10). How does one run but by seeking and praying? "I will run the way of thy commandments," (Psalm 119:32), given as a runner in the duties of holiness, which is what the commandments point to. Christ secures and defends His people from the rage of Satan by His covenant work. Satan's rage is called his fiery darts, and the malice and persecutions of wicked men. Christ's protection, like the refreshing shade of an Apple Tree, is round about them, called a shield and relieving shadow: "Thou hast been a shadow from the heat", (Isaiah 25:4). It is there in Christ that is the Christian's only sanctuary. "When I am afraid," David says, "I will trust in thee," (Psalm 56:3). The weight of that word in trusting God is likened to a refuge in the time of a hurricane. In the most difficult of times, Christ is the *Hedge of Protection*. Those who dwell in His heavenly habitation are preserved from a dead, frozen, and numbing frame of spirit. They are set on fire by God's Spirit, made zealous, fervent in spirit, serving the Lord, inflamed with a divine fervor (by the influence of the Holy Spirit, which is likened to fire), animating them with courage and resolution to stand for God and His ways against all the opposition of evil that might come their way. Christ is the Christian's chief comfort in tribulation, the joy and delight of his soul. He is the chief good in Himself, and in Him is the saints' treasure laid up; with Him is the most desirable communion and safety, even though the world, the flesh, and the devil rage against them. "Whom have I in heaven but thee, and there is none on earth that I desire besides thee," Asaph says (Psalm 73:25). This is why sinners are bid to come and rest in Him. The world is a very unrestful place, because Satan is a very unrestful spirit, filled with all manner of malice against sinners. But Christ is a Christian's home. A sinner may be said to be wandering in the wilderness of the world, liable to all temptations when they are absent from Christ's near presence, and when they stray from the righteous course, giving full reins to a loose, carnal, and dissolute mind pursuing the vanities and follies of the world, neglecting the solid comforts and delights of his proper home, exposing himself to the hazards of a strange and dangerous entertainment among his soul-enemies. The world, the flesh, and the devil are his soul-enemies. To live to God, which is the end of all theological ideas, in a way of spiritual love and communion, is to dwell in Christ. The Lord Jesus is the only way that leads to this strong tower, for as He says, "I am the way, the truth, and the life, no man cometh to the Father but by me." He is the sanctuary, the altar, the priest, all of it, for His saints, and the petition is relevant to it all: "Deliver us Lord Jesus from the evil one." Be that safe and retreating place from the assaults of Satan, sin, and in-bred corruption. From these enemies there is no safety, but by flying to the mercy of God in Christ.

The blood of Christ in all this is a *Fountain of life* (Revelation 21:6), a fountain opened for sin and for uncleanness (Zechariah 13:1). If the Christian is not watchful in this, and does not dwell as such in Christ in this way of watching and praying, they are in a very sad and dismal condition, being exposed to the malice of their soul-enemies without a shield or a strong tower. They are ignorant of the devices used against them, the work of the Spirit that they have not harnessed well for their good. Christ teaches His people how to behave themselves in spiritual conflicts, and to fight under His banner (Psalm 18:34) when He calls them to His service. He warns them of the dangers of enemies, and discovers the subtleties and devices of their soul-adversaries. Thomas Brooks' work, *Precious Remedies Against Satan's*

Devices, has 12 devices to study of the devil and his work in the Christian's life.

Device (1): To present the bait and hide the hook; to present the golden cup, and hide the poison; to present the sweet, the pleasure, and the profit that may flow in upon the soul by yielding to sin, and by hiding from the soul the wrath and misery that will certainly follow the committing of sin.[24] Device (9): By presenting to the soul the crosses, losses, reproaches, sorrows, and sufferings that do daily attend those that walk in the ways of holiness.[25] Christians do not understand the great tools they have at their disposal where the Lord is a wall of fire round about His people: "For I, saith the LORD, will be unto her a wall of fire round about, and will be the glory in the midst of her", (Zechariah 2:5). What a hedge it is, that Satan himself takes notice of it (Job 1:10), and no battering ram can make a breach in, and no ladder can scale it. There is no fighting against Christ, for He is too hard a match for any spiritual enemy against His people. The world, the flesh, and the devil make desperate and foolish attempts to attack this fort of Christ in believers, for it is impregnable; it cannot be overtaken. But the Christian can give into such attacks

---

[24] Thomas Brooks, The Complete Works of Thomas Brooks, ed. Alexander Balloch Grosart, vol. 1 (Edinburgh; London; Dublin: James Nichol; James Nisbet and Co.; G. Herbert, 1866), 12.
[25] Thomas Brooks, The Complete Works of Thomas Brooks, ed. Alexander Balloch Grosart, vol. 1 (Edinburgh; London; Dublin: James Nichol; James Nisbet and Co.; G. Herbert, 1866), 47.

by wandering outside that strong tower. Yes, the Christian knows, even on a basic level, what sin is, and its defiling and damning quality. They are not ignorant of Satan's devices, by which he labors to bypass them; they see the weakness of their spiritual enemies, and they do not fear them, so long as this Tower encloses them, and this Hedge is round about them. How will they be sure of it but to pray "deliver us from evil"? God keeps off the blows and fiery darts of the devil, from wounding that part or grace of the soul which is in the greatest danger when temptations and attacks come forth. Sometimes Satan strikes at the faith of a Christian, and so God appears by His Word and Spirit for the strengthening of that. Sometimes Satan strikes at the grace of God's love to His people; God then presents immediately divine objects to the soul in the means of grace, and shows it, more and more, the deformity and emptiness of this world, and by it increases and preserves the love of the soul to Himself, and to Jesus Christ.

Sometimes Satan aims at the will of the Christian, where some temptations are laid to catch that will and make them refuse self-denial. Such a temptation comes very forcibly, when it runs with the surge of their own wills, when it is to save themselves, their livelihood, their children, from the danger of the world. The devil will speak to the Christian, "What? Will you serve Christ, when he frustrates you in everything? That which is tangible has so much more to offer you. What? Follow God, and yield to such hard terms he gives you as to be in denial of your whole self and give him everything?" Consider it, that any sin runs along that course. But Christ has already showed the Christian that His will, which is far better, should be done rather than their own. The Christian will lose nothing by doing anything for His sake, rather the opposite. And because heavenly rewards seem intangible, Satan is often most against them, the world does not recognize them, and the flesh would rather be fulfilled now in passion than in patience. Do Christians have need to pray "Deliver us from evil"? God says, "I am thy Shield," as much as if He should say, "I will defend and save you from all the darts and arrows of your enemies." By this Shield, every faculty of the soul, and grace of the Spirit is preserved. Christ and His work and merit is the defense and security of His people from the devil, that roaring Lion, and old red Dragon; and from the world, in its cruel, brutish, devouring, and merciless dispositions, which are compared to lions, bears, and such. God is a Wall of Fire, as a hedge and defense of His people if they would just pray and look to Him, be on watch and guard and look to Him, use the Spirit powers they have availed to them to be delivered from evil.

While they remain in the howling wilderness of this world, where their danger is very great, there being multitudes of temptations and difficulties, beasts, monsters, devils ready to destroy them. *The 1647 Westminster Larger Catechism Question 195* asks: What do we pray for in the sixth petition?

> Answer: In the sixth petition (which is, And lead us not into temptation, but deliver us from evil), acknowledging, that the most wise, righteous, and gracious God, for divers holy and just ends, may so order things, that we may be assaulted, foiled, and for a time led captive by temptations; that Satan, the world, and the flesh, are ready powerfully to draw us aside, and ensnare us; and that we, even after the pardon of our sins, by reason of our corruption, weakness, and want of watchfulness, are not only subject to be tempted, and forward to expose ourselves unto temptations, but also of ourselves unable and unwilling to resist them, to recover out of them, and to improve them; and worthy to be left under the power of them: we pray, that God would so overrule the world and all in it, subdue the flesh, and restrain Satan, order all things, bestow and bless all means of grace, and quicken us to watchfulness in the use of them, that we and all his people may by his providence be kept from being tempted to sin; or, if tempted, that by his Spirit we may be powerfully supported and enabled to stand in the hour of temptation; or

> when fallen, raised again and recovered out of it, and have a sanctified use and improvement thereof: that our sanctification and salvation may be perfected, Satan trodden under our feet, and we fully freed from sin, temptation, and all evil, forever. Christians pray not to be kept under the power of the devil and delivered from the times of trial that evil brings. And they keep watch and pray daily to that end.

We pray, that God would *either* keep us from being tempted to sin, or support and deliver us when we are tempted, (as the *Shorter Catechism question 106 also declares)*. Anything that is hurtful to your souls you are to pray daily against. You have a promise annexed to it: "God is faithful, who will not suffer you to be tempted above that ye are able; but will with the temptation also make a way to escape, that ye may be able to bear it," (1 Corinthians 10:13). Can't He just deliver us? He does through Christ. But no, I mean, I just don't want the temptation at all. Hope for heaven in that, it is not what the petition means. It is only in heaven that such will be experienced. Here is not the case. Know that it is part of God's faithfulness to keep you from evil, and to moderate and mitigate temptation to your strength. God suits the temptation to your ability. So, temptations become more difficult and more subtle or crafty as you age in Christian maturity. He will keep you from the evil of sin, so far as it is damning, and death in that respect. He will keep you from a sin that leads to death (1 John 5:16). He will help you that it will not reign in your mortal bodies, since you are dead to it: "For sin shall not have dominion over you: for ye are not under the Law, but under grace," (Romans 6:14).

But it is not a final deliverance now of such things. It will only be a final deliverance from temptation when you arrive in heaven. That idea is *implied* in the petition.

Do you not desire that place where there is no sorrow, no sin, no more assaults on you from Satan or anything that defiles, that we may be kept from all wickedness? You are to go to Christ now for deliverance, by prayer and watchfulness, "deliver us from evil." And you are not so concerned just for yourself, but as it is in all of the petitions, not only are they daily, but that they are for "us," for the church, for the family of Christ. It places you in mind not only for your own sins, but for the sanctification of the whole church of Christ. Not only that you be kept from the evil of temptation, but that the whole church would be kept from the trouble and devices of the devil. The petition moves you to consider how God directs you in the course of this life. It teaches you how to submit to God's providence, and how to go about gaining mercy and power in the midst of it. God does not exempt you from tribulation and instead makes all tribulation sanctifying to you. How many times will a person go through a certain temptation and yield to it, to learn nothing of it, and to continue to go through it because they learned nothing of it? He will support you in His mercy, but how many times will you deal with the same thing over and over and *never learn* and keep falling into what you do not want to do, and still do, over and over? For some it shows their hypocrisy; for a Christian, though, it shows the world, the flesh, and the devil know how to push their buttons in just the right way, at just the right time, at opportune times, to cause them to give heed to that which has no positive profit, but may yield some negative profit.

When a young Christian is born again, they learn positively what to do and do not have to untwist old habits. Older Christians who are converted at an older age have to relearn all kinds of things, and take off old habits that are very hard to take off; instead of merely learning new ones. If a Christian, then, time and time again falls into the same sins, the same temptation in the same ways without ever peeling back the layers of the onion to find out what is at its core, they are impacted negatively because they have to deal with it and time and time again they deal with the same things they have to unlearn. They are not learning the lessons they must, in order to be radical against the world, the flesh, and the devil to deal with being delivered from sin in the way God has ordained. He rescues them from the mouth of the lion or paw of the bear, and yet the next day there they are back in the wilderness wandering around again. He rescues them from the mouth of the lion and yet, the next day they are back in the wilderness, again.

You might say, is that person *even* a Christian? Maybe not, maybe so, for Christians, they are imperfect in this world, and they will sin while the old man is still with them, and they must use all the tools and weapons at their disposal to overcome and be more than conquerors; and yet, Christians will wander; which is why this is a daily prayer. This teaches you how to wait and hope for the end of your prayers by exercising what God has given you in Christ and in the Spirit. *Pray that ye enter not into temptation*; yet not just that, but be kept from evil; that whatever way you are tempted and tried in God's providence, you come forth learning in Christ's school what you are to learn. What a terrible thing it is for Christians to deal with the *same* sins, over and over again that the devil throws their way because they keep missing a vital point of warfare. Imagine a general who keeps sending the same people in the same way into the same strait only to have the same outcome time and time again occur, that all the soldiers but one return to report that they are overwhelmed and the rest died. People would think that general mad to keep doing the same thing and expecting a different result. And yet, Christians seem to do it *all the time*. Same sins, same way, same times, over and over, with no change in behavior on that sin; they'll *pray*, because that to them is *easy*.

Some sins they do, that they do not even know they have done them, and are secret faults, never having turned over that rock to find out if what they did is a sin or not. "Examine yourselves, whether ye be in the faith; prove your own selves. Know ye not your own selves, how that Jesus Christ is in you, except ye be reprobates?" (2 Corinthians 13:5). Satan knows you, do you know yourselves? How can you be informed of his devices without examination?

From such ideas, we may infer the necessity of self-examination in this, in other words, whether we have any *interest* in really being delivered from evil. If we dwell in love to God (1 John 4:16; Deuteronomy 11:1), then we dwell in God; for to love Him is to keep His commandments. This love must be with all our hearts, and to Him above all others, for He will have no competitor. A serious return from wandering in the wilderness of the world for sins and temptations to be abated and a hearty renunciation of the devil's devices denotes an interest in Christ and His world over all things. And so, from this we infer the absolute necessity of a self-examination in this. How might we obtain victory over the world and the flesh and the devil, by first praying "deliver us from evil," as it pertains to us and to our church, considering how many evil beasts are watching to devour us, and the impending storms that threaten us, in such perilous days as we live in? That we ought to be very circumspect in our walking, in our course, which this petition implies. That we are not turned out of the way, nor lose our hopes and assurance of the right way, nor be discouraged in the way. You know you will have tribulations, you are promised them, so what is the outcome? Christians pray not to be kept under the power of the devil and delivered from the times of trial that evil brings. Pray in this way:

> Lord, you see how our enemies, the world, the flesh, and the devil, are every moment soliciting, enticing, alluring, or tempting us to evil. Be merciful to us, save, and help, and deliver us. You see how weak I am, and how ready my own deceitful heart is, to surrender itself to the Tempter; and I know that Satan cannot tempt me without your permission, or mine. Do not lead me if it is your good pleasure, do not allow me to fall into violent or lasting temptations, that may endanger my perseverance. I know that to be tempted is not sin, for your own beloved Son, God incarnate, was tempted to the most horrid of all sins, to fall down and worship the very devil. I know Lord, the sin lies in yielding to the Temptation. O my God, if you try my love, and lead me into any great temptation, and let me continue under such temptations, your will be

done, not mine. But let your tenderness limit and control the Tempter. Let your all-sufficient grace restrain my consent, and keep me always on my guard, watching and praying, and let me at last be more than a conqueror in Christ. I am content, Lord, to be tried and assaulted, so that I am not wicked, though it is grievous for those that love you, to be tempted to offend you. O Father of mercy, if you think it fit to lead me into temptation, deliver me from the evil to which I am tempted. Deliver me from the evil of sin, and the evil of punishment, from the evil one, from the evil world, and from my own evil heart, and from all suggestions to evil, for all that is evil is most hateful to you, who are infinite goodness, and most destructive of your love. And therefore from all that is evil, O Almighty Lord defend me.

In the next chapter we will conclude the prayer in the *doxology*.

Chapter 9: Thine is the Kingdom

The Lord's Prayer concludes with a majestic *crescendo* in Matthew 6:13c: "For thine is the kingdom, and the power, and the glory, for ever. Amen." Some of the more ancient texts add this doxology, "For thine is the kingdom and the power and the glory forever, Amen." It is to be noted that some ancient manuscripts do *not* include it. But simply because some do not have it when Matthew was originally written does not mean that Matthew was unaware of it, or that it was not being used. Quite the opposite. Not only was it being used, and therefore known, and may not need to have been regularly added into the script, but some of them do have it, and *all* the manuscripts should be considered.

It is a wonderful ending to this prayer in praise. It is doxological, which is important. This conclusion was left out in the Lord's Prayer in Luke, but in Matthew 6 it is present in accordance with David's benediction in 1 Chronicles 29:11–13: "Thine, O LORD, is the greatness, and the power, and the glory, and the victory, and the majesty: for all that is in the heaven and in the earth is thine; thine is the kingdom, O LORD, and thou art exalted as head above all. Both riches and honour come of thee, and thou reignest over all; and in thine hand is power and might; and in thine hand it is to make great, and to give strength unto all. Now therefore, our God, we thank thee, and praise thy glorious name." This prayer was part of David's prayer as it concerned the building of the temple, the place of God's *nearness*. In this way, the conclusion teaches that the ground and end of all the believer's prayers is for the purpose of God's kingdom and power, the end being God's eternal glory. Such a prayer is doxological.

Doxology is a matter of praise and of glorifying God; to give glory to Him. There is a great stress set on praising the Father, praising God, for redemption, and giving Him an adoration of His supreme excellence as He is in heaven, which name should echo the heavenly state of being holy, here on earth. The doxology is set within the framework of a personal understanding of praise and prayer and how they are so linked together. Prayer and praise are intrinsically linked together and provide, often, fuel for one another. One theologian likened prayer and praise to a bird's two wings that work in harmony together. The doxology is linked by the conjunction "for": "for thine is the kingdom and the power and the glory." Kingdom *and* power both describe the same idea surrounding God's governance and ruling of both the world *and* the church. Such a use of this phrase is what is called a *hendiadys*, a figure of speech in which two words connected by a conjunction are used to express a single notion that would normally be expressed by an adjective and a substantive, such as grace and favor instead of saying gracious favor. It is common in ancient literature to see this. The thought here is of omnipotent sovereign power in Christ's governance and control of all things. Kingdom is used as in Psalm 103:19, "His kingdom rules over all." Such a kingdom (*Spirit-influence*) signifies God's governance and providence of the order of creation. This in turn is assumed by the petition that God's kingdom may "come" in its fullness. The former petitions rest in these final words.

One should not think that God's will is open for debate. God's will *does not change*. The *Ten Commandments* do not change. It was asked in the beginning of the study, if God already knows, then *why* pray? It is that the believer prays to align his will with God's, and that God will answer his requests as they line up with His will. "Kingdom" here is based on the Spirit-influenced age of Christ. That Christ is all-sufficient to do all things in His governance over all people, especially His church, by which His kingdom is an invading, fall-reversing power into the current worldview. It is Christ's sovereign right as King to rule all things from heaven in His kingdom. He is able, by His sovereign power, to bring all things under His governance under His absolute subjection. It comprises both His providence and His church. He governs all things in His providence, and He governs His church by His word and Spirit. The Kingdom is God's, "Thine." It is God's Kingdom, and all His prescriptions are to be followed in it for His glory. Christ is differentiated from any earthly king who gains power, whereby Christ, being God, is power, and His Kingdom is His own. Even in regard to God allowing Satan to have a kingdom of darkness, God uses the devil for His glorious purposes, to His own glory, and for the good of His church. "Thine is the power" refers to God's ability to do, as Sovereign, whatsoever He decrees to come to pass. Whatever God's will is, so His power is, and where God wills something, He has the power to do that something. "And the glory" is His weightiness or nearness of His presence in all His excellence and majesty, set to work for the glory of His own being, in His Kingdom. Amen is translated as the final, let it be so, to all of this sensible praying.

The doctrine to consider, in conclusion of the Lord's Prayer, teaches that those who pray, praise Him, ascribing kingdom, power, and glory to Him. That may seem *obvious*, but what does it *mean*, for prayer and praise are two parts linked by a common thread, to give glory to God. Christians are to take their encouragement in prayer only from God, who is able to bring to pass those things that Christians have prayed for in aligning their will to His. Christians in their prayers are to praise Him, ascribing kingdom (glorious rule), power (omnipotence), and glory to Him (the weightiness of His presence). Christians in testimony of their desire, and assurance to be heard, say, *Amen*.

First, Christians are to take their encouragement in prayer by trusting God. Vain babbling, which Christ previously disdained as useless, achieves nothing. To merely make a prayer is drudgery, and not an exercise in praise and prayer makes prayer itself to be quite hard. And people think that if one prays enough, and long enough, and repeats such things, over and over again in some mantra-like form, that God will pay attention to them and answer their petitions. This is not what prayer is. Christians pray knowing God is at work, and that their desires, in the way they express the Lord's Prayer, is to align *their* wills with *His*. It does not change God's will, but aligns God's decrees with the Christian's prayers as they pray His will from His word. They know He is the sovereign King, and they know all His works come to pass; they conform their will to His known will. The Christian's prayer is offered in faith, and such is based on what they know to be true about God. If they do not know God is sovereign, or that He receives all the glory, or is all-sufficient in Himself to accomplish all His intended ends against all that ever or will ever occur, it would be quite needless to pray. They would have no sense of God ever answering anything if all their prayers were *just on a whim*. Such prayers they pray righteously are aligned with God's will already, and such are co-extensive with God's decrees that are already in motion, and so they presume such prayers are prayed for His glory. These prayers come from a true faith, based on God's word, and they emerge from the heart, and are believed to be effectual where God in His sovereignty will answer accordingly.

If the heart is cheerful in its prayers, and links to prayers the praiseworthiness of God, then one is praying in accordance with both the Lord's Prayer and the *Psalms*. Consider how the Psalms are often *not very long*, bring like-petitions as the Lord's Prayer, and then include *doxology*. Where did Jesus get this Lord's Prayer but by the Scriptures, teaching what has always been the case, and how the people of God have always prayed and relied on God as the sovereign King? Are they not praying about a Kingdom, is it not His Kingdom? To have a Kingdom implies not only a King, but an all-sufficient and sovereign one who rules it. Whereas, those who deny Jesus Christ as our only sovereign and Lord, as Jude says, are wayward and lost and have no idea what it means to pray in the Holy Spirit; most people think praying in the Holy Spirit is babbling in some unknown tongue for long lengths of time. The Christian who is serious in his intentions and takes pleasure in prayer does not come to prayer hoping to be able to make long arduous prayers for the sake of doing so, or to babble. Luther said, insightfully, "God does not ask how much and how long you have prayed, but how good the prayer is and whether it proceeds from the heart."[26] Jesus said, "Your heavenly Father knows what you need before you ask for it." Paul even says, "We do not know how we are to pray", (Romans 8:26). Is prayer all about instructing Christ what He ought to do for the Christian from His throne, and His kingdom? Or is it that God desires *His people* to know what He is *already* doing for His church, He is already engaged in His work, and they are to pray in such a way that His name might be hallowed, His kingdom extended, and His will advanced? They are to simply *align* their wills with His; they are cognizant of what God says they need according to His word, for He already knows all things, and so they *align* their wills with His. This allows His people to recognize and confess that He is already working, and does work, for the good of His people, for His glory. Praise and prayer are intrinsically linked in this way in that prayer fuels the realization that the Christian has of what God is doing, and then when their heart is sensible of such things, they then praise Him for His acts. This is the basis for high thoughts of God.

But what thoughts will the Christian have if they do not understand what they are doing when they pray, or that prayer becomes drudgery, or long-windedness thinking they can turn God's will to them rather than

---

[26] Martin Luther, Luther's Works, Vol. 21: The Sermon on the Mount and the Magnificat, ed. Jaroslav Jan Pelikan, Hilton C. Oswald, and Helmut T. Lehmann, vol. 21 (Saint Louis: Concordia Publishing House, 1999), 143.

have their will turn to His? The Christian heart learns daily to be submissive to God from the time they spend in gaining the fuel they need for prayer in the word of God. They come to realize He must increase and they must decrease, and acknowledge all is in His hands. As the ditty goes, He has the whole world in His hands. They look to Him for everything and expect everything that concerns His kingdom, power, and glory to be ascribed to Him forever.

Christians in their prayers are to praise Him, ascribing kingdom, power, and glory to Him. What then does sensible prayer in this light comprise so that prayer turns to praise and praise turns to prayer? The first part of the prayer, because He is "our Father," declares that He should receive the glory due to Him, because His name should be held in high reverence and honor in the church and throughout the world, to be regarded as holy. All false doctrine, all false worship, all false ideas of every kind are condemned here. All heretics are silenced by it, all those who profane His name are silenced in it, and such opposes all that is false, in opposition to His commandments. Then such petitions in word and truth are extended into the Kingdom of God, which is all-encompassing, that there should be a furtherance and expansion of the Kingdom and of the Spirit's influence. When Christians pray to be more serviceable, or more like Christ, or more holy, they are praying for Kingdom expansion. That Christ as King govern over all the world, and all the church, which He does. That His will would be the Christian's will. That He then would guard that strong tower against the wiles of the world, the flesh, and the devil. This is prayed so that His will would be accomplished by the Spirit, by Christ, by His decree, in the world.

It is an interesting notion that the will of God and His decrees often operate in *tandem* with the prayers of the saints. Christians know the Kingship of Christ, in that He does not only provide for their spiritual well-being, but their physical well-being, one necessarily giving way for the other to operate. If a person is physically dead, the spiritual desires of the saint cannot take place as it is outlined in such a sensible prayer; he must be living and walking and talking and breathing. They need things that apply to their daily life: daily bread—everything necessary for the preservation of this life: all things temporal. And annexed to this is also everything kept at bay which may occur like war, pestilence, sickness, and such. Then, that God would forgive His people their debts, so that they also consider how to treat others. They have *commandments* that surround neighbors. How shall they treat those that sin against them? How will they help those in need? Then that God would govern their life as they live in the fall, and deal with the kingdom of darkness: they fight against the world, the flesh, and the devil. They have all kinds of temptations and troubles, "you will have tribulation." They do not go a minute without God's help. They desire to be utterly and completely delivered from all the forces of darkness whatsoever they are. All their needs are brought to Him, as they are outlined in the Prayer, in the word.

And then what? "For Thine is the kingdom and the power and the glory, forever." Christ presses the need for the Christian to give a doxology by recognizing in each of these petitions that they pray, their reliance on God to govern them well according to righteousness, to judge all things for them according to righteousness, and to bring glory to Himself in His help of His bride. It is the doxology of His kingship; Scripture is filled with God as Sovereign King—you know, the Gospel. It is a confession and praise and prayer of "Our God reigns."

I'll say it a million times more, get the sovereignty of God wrong, and *all theological ideas fall apart*; in fact, get sovereignty wrong, and one cannot even pray, which is why Jude says that men who creep into the church with false ideas about Christ's not being sovereign are heretical and damned, deemed *ungodly* (Jude 1:4). What does that say about the greater part of professing Christendom? God rules and reigns and triumphs, and the prayers of the saints attest to it, being sensible of His ruling and reigning. His "kingdom" is His sovereign reign, one thing given for another. It is a *metonymy*, kingdom is given for sovereignty, and power is given for the execution of that authority which He exercises. In the same way, "the glory" is a *metonymy*, given for the end of His exercise of power in His kingdom, for His honor or praise; this belonging only to the Triune God in Christ. To give one thing is to give the others; to ascribe power to God is to ascribe glory, to ascribe glory is to ascribe sovereignty, they are all wrapped up in one sovereignty of ruling. Wherever there is God's authority and power, equally, all the glory and all the praise belong to Him,. for it derives from Him and is for Him and to Him. Here is the Lord's Prayer again: "For of him, and through him, and to him, are all things: to whom be glory for ever. Amen," (Romans 11:36). It is the same thing. His kingdom, power, and glory triumph throughout the church and the world.

Christians know they are not worthy, and yet they have the ear of God. They take encouragement in prayer, not from themselves or any worthiness of their own but from God alone, who having such eternal sovereignty and power and all sufficiency, having the glory forever, in His work of His kingdom, is incomparably glorious in His faithfulness and goodness to His people who are sensible of it. Take it this way, those who are sensible of this aspect of praying the prayer, and praising Him for His power, gain more from prayer than merely sending up a barrage of words. That does not mean those barrages of words from a Christian are not heard, but it may mean the Spirit must take those words and bring the lawful petitions before the throne, discarding those things that would be nonetheless, useless so to speak. "We do not present our supplications for our righteousness, but for thy great mercies. O Lord hear; O Lord, forgive; O Lord, hearken, and do defer not, for thine own sake, O my God," (Daniel 9:18–19). Daniel 9:4–19 was his prayer, and God sent Gabriel to answer some question for him. The Psalmist said, "Hearken unto the voice of my cry, my King, and my God; for unto thee will I pray," (Psalm 5:2). How will he pray? Psalm 5 is 12 verses. "Now unto him that is able to do exceeding abundantly above all that we ask or think, according to the power that worketh in us, Unto him be glory in the Church by Christ Jesus throughout all ages, world without end. Amen", (Ephesians 3:20, 21). That is a short *doxology*. This is not meant to dissuade Christians from longer prayer, but to discern the sensible need for the *quality* of their prayer before God. This one fellow said to me, "I think that God hears prayer more, after we spend time in prayer, at least an hour in prayer." That's *nonsense*; how long was Psalm 5 or 12, or 23, or Daniel's prayer? And yet, *sensibly*, Luther said, *I'm so busy today I think I will spend another hour with God.* If needs be, do so. But it is not by vain ramblings that one is heard, for their many words, Jesus says. And if prayer does not fuel praise, and they are not linked, how much of prayer has been left off? That little acronym, ACTS? Adoration, confession, thanksgiving, supplication is a bit oversimplistic, but, note, adoration is set for the "A".

In prayer God is to be praised for what the Christian knows is true about Him according to His word. They are to ascribe to Him praise according to His kingdom, power, and glory: "Now unto the King eternal, immortal, invisible, the only wise God, be honour and glory for ever and ever. Amen," (1 Timothy 1:18).

Let's finally consider a short mention of the word AMEN. Christians in testimony of their desire, and assurance to be heard, say, *Amen*; then is this ending to the Lord's Prayer, the doxological testimony. AMEN is a Hebrew word which is a verbal adjective connected with a root signifying to *make firm*, or to *establish*. This is done with *certainty*, with *assent*. Its function is associated with worship, prayer, the expression of will and desire, and attached primarily to doxological ideas of praise. It is almost entirely found in connection with prayers, doxologies, or benedictions: "Blessed be the LORD God of Israel from everlasting to everlasting: and let all the people say, Amen. Praise ye the LORD," (Psalm 106:48). "And Ezra blessed the LORD, the great God. And all the people answered, Amen, Amen, with lifting up their hands: and they bowed their heads, and worshipped the LORD with their faces to the ground," (Nehemiah 8:6). "Else when thou shalt bless with the spirit, how shall he that occupieth the room of the unlearned say Amen at thy giving of thanks, seeing he understandeth not what thou sayest?" (1 Corinthians 14:16). Even the unlearned should be able, in *doxology*, to say *Amen* to the doxology, to *praise*. Jerome has a reference to the loud congregational "Amen," which he describes as resounding like thunder ('*ad similitudinem cœlestis tonitrui*'—Com. ad Galat.); this corresponds to a synagogue custom of uttering the 'Amen with the full power' of the voice.[27] Christians end prayers of all kinds with the word "Amen," setting forth the idea that which signifies so be it or so shall it be; in Christ's name, by His power, and kingdom, AMEN. This is a word of testimony. To testify of something is to bear witness of any person or thing by word or work. For God, as an example, the whole of His word is a testimony to His sovereign work, the whole Scripture or Word of God is a testimony from God: "The testimony of the Lord is sure, and giveth wisdom unto the simple," (Psalm 19:7). Or His commandments are set in the same light, the two Tables of Stone, in which the Law was written: "And he took, and put the Testimony in the Ark," (Exodus 40:20; cf. Exodus 25:16, 31, 31:18). The *testimony* of Jesus Christ is the Gospel of Christ. Revelation 1:9 and 12:17 call the Gospel His *testimony*. Because it is revealed by Christ, in regard of which He is called the faithful witness (Revelation 1:5); and none could open the scroll except He (Revelation 4:9). The subject of this testimony is Christ, or the doctrine of faith and salvation fashioned

---

[27] Shab. 119b, J. S. Clemens, "Amen," ed. James Hastings, A Dictionary of Christ and the Gospels: Aaron–Zion (Edinburgh; New York: T&T Clark; Charles Scribner's Sons, 1906), 52.

by Christ alone (Romans 1:2). Such was testified to by Christ; not only revealing it by His divine doctrine, but also by His holy life, mighty miracles, faithful profession before the Jews, Pharisees, Pontius Pilate, the whole Council, and by His innocent death. Because the end of such a testimony aims at His glory (Acts 2:36); the aim is doxological. To have this testimony, to give credence to it is to testify of it. To profess the Gospel, to uphold and maintain it, to give witness to it, and to hold it in life and death as in Revelation 20:4 as it is said of those martyred for Christ's glory.

AMEN sets forth a word of testimony to the truth of what is being *concurred* with. When one's will is aligned with God's will and then given credence, in testimony of their desires and assurances to be heard, they say, "Amen"; let it be so—AMEN is not "we are done praying" but "we agree and testify to the truth of the prayer that it be done." At the end of prayer, it is a desire that such may be so, and a trusting that it shall be so. It is sometimes the title of God Himself, and of Christ, because of His faithfulness and truth, in performing all promises (Revelation 3:14; Isaiah 65:16). It is a Hebrew word, not translated into Greek, but is used in all languages. It is set squarely by the Christian in his prayer, in his ending of praise to God, of the truth which it signifies: so be it (Jeremiah 11:5). It is a note of affirmation, or confirming a thing to be. How could such be done by the Christian if they are *unsure* of what God will do? But they can be sure of what God will do by a *knowledge of His word* in which He says what He shall do, and what He does do, and they are sensible of this. And so, the end of the prayer turns to a confirmation of their consent both in a thing to be confirmed and hoped on. It is a Christian's great praise to consent to the truth, Christ faithfully fulfilling His promises, which are all "yea and Amen," (Revelation 3:14). This is the sealing and final word of the prayer prayed.

Is it not a comfort? "I wonder if I have prayed in a way that God is hearing me?" Do you even think about that? The Lord's Prayer dispels that question entirely; you never have to wonder if you pray as Jesus instructed. It's not about repeating the prayer mechanically, but praying it in a way that expounds your desires, which align with God's desires and follow His word. You have a holy Father in heaven, King through His Son, trustworthy and working for your good, giving you confidence. This Father, with His Kingdom, power, and aim for His own glory, assures you He attends all your prayers, even when you falter and the Spirit intercedes with groans on your behalf. His power guarantees He can help you. Christ is the great Sovereign King, and as your King, He is eager to aid you in all troubles or needs: "Casting all your care upon him; for he careth for you," (1 Peter 5:7). People often misinterpret this as license to say whatever comes to mind, improvising freely. No, it's right here, in the sensible praying Christ gave. As with

His commandments, His prayer covers everything. It teaches you to draw near to God with holy reverence and confidence, as children to a Father, able and ready to help; and to pray with and for others. It teaches you to pray that God would enable you and others to glorify Him in all He reveals Himself to be; and that He would dispose all things to His glory. It teaches you to pray that Satan's kingdom be destroyed; that the kingdom of grace be advanced, yourselves and others brought into it and kept in it; and that the kingdom of glory by Spirit-influence be hastened to come fully. It teaches you that God, by His grace, would make you able and willing to know, obey, and submit to His will in all things, as they do in heaven. It teaches you to pray for a sufficient portion of this life's good things, enjoying God's blessing with them. It teaches you that God, for Christ's sake, would freely pardon all your sins, encouraging you to ask because His grace enables you to forgive others from the heart. It teaches you that God would keep you from being tempted to sin, or support and deliver you when tempted.

What an encouragement that in every situation—spiritual, tangible, temporary, or eternal—He teaches you to draw encouragement from God alone. As a result, in your prayers, you praise Him, ascribing kingdom, power, and glory to Him; and, in testimony of your desire and assurance to be heard, you say, Amen. What glorifies Him more than showing mercy to His people by hearing their prayers and aiding them in distress? "I will hear thee, and thou shalt glorify my name", (Psalm 50:15). Such giving of thanks, attached to all those petitions, mirrors heaven's worship: "Thou art worthy, O Lord, to receive honor, and glory, and power," (Revelation 4:9, 11). Paul says, "Be distrustful in nothing, but in all things let your requests be made known to God with giving of thanks", (Philippians 4:6). It is commanded, for Jesus was not merely speaking to be heard. Prayer must be accompanied by thanksgiving. All of it—King, power, and glory—is a sound summation of all the Psalms of praise. That's why Christ used David's praise as the cornerstone of His conclusion in teaching His disciples to pray: "Thine O Lord is greatness, and power, and glory, and victory, and praise; for all that is in heaven and earth is thine; thine is the kingdom, O Lord, and thou excellest as head over all; both riches and honor come from thee, and thou reignest over all; and in thine hand is power, and strength, etc." (1 Chronicles 29:11–12). It is no accident that Christ begins the prayer ascribing glory to God in hallowing His name and ends with ascribing glory by testimony.

When you glorify God by being *satisfied* in Him and pray this prayer *in* such satisfaction, you link it to praise. "I am not worthy of the least of all the mercies, and of all the truth which thou hast showed unto thy servant," (Genesis 32:10); so, "To thee, O Lord, belongeth righteousness, but unto us open shame," (Daniel 9:7).

You pray the doxological praise, desiring God's name to be hallowed in all your petitions, that He would help you believe He works for your good, giving comfort in all your requests. How should this part of the prayer be prayed?

> "I adore, and love you, Jesus, that the right end of my prayer should be your glory of God, and that I ought to mix praise with my prayers, and to be as zealous to give thanks for what I receive, as to pray for what I desire. On you alone we rely and depend for acceptance, to you alone we offer up our praises, for thine is the Kingdom and Sovereign right to dispose of all things; thine is the power Almighty, to relieve and bless us, thine is the glory. All, the communications of your goodness, as they flow from you to your bride, return to you again in sacrifices of love, of praise, and adoration. For the sake of your beloved, in whom all your promises are Amen, and who is himself the Amen, the faithful and true Witness of your love to us. Hear me, and pardon my wanderings and coldness, and help me to sum up and seal my whole prayer; all my own needs, and all the needs of those I pray for, in a hearty and fervent, and comprehensive, AMEN."

There is a caveat in this because if a person does not believe that Christ is *truly* King, how will he pray? If Christ is not regarded as the *sovereign* King, over a *sovereign* Kingdom, and if the Gospel is not "Our God reigns" through the work and merit of Jesus Christ, *can* a person pray? If God is your King, will you obey Him and honor all His commandments? The prayer and the commandments are *intrinsically* linked together. Without the commandments, the prayers don't make much sense. Without the knowledge that Christ is King, the entire Lord's Prayer turns to *something else*. If God is King of the kingdom of grace, it should humble you to pray in a manner consistent with His *Kingship*. That would color your prayers in a certain way.

Those who are not obedient to the great King show they really have no comfort in His kingdom. In the parable of the Ten Pounds, the Lord Jesus concludes, "But those mine enemies, which would not that I should reign over them, bring hither, and slay them before me," (Luke 19:27). It is the great sin of the day in the church of Jesus Christ, that Christians have issue with Christ's *government*; they will *not* have Christ reign over them as King. They are happy to have Him as Savior, but not as Lord God almighty with power who rules His Kingdom by His commandments. They quickly forget, "He that hath my commandments, and keepeth them, he it is that loveth me: and he that loveth me shall be loved of my

Father, and I will love him, and will manifest myself to him," (John 14:21). As if to say, he it is that acknowledges me as King over them.

You have no recourse to pray in any way without acknowledging Christ as Sovereign King. Not just King, but *Sovereign* King. What is prayer without knowledge—it is impossible, really. Young Christians can pray, but knowledgeable Christians have opportunity to pray *more* widely and effectively. The Psalmist prays this way: "Happy is he that hath the God of Jacob for his help, whose hope is in the LORD his God: which made heaven and earth, the sea, and all that therein is: which keepeth truth for ever: which executeth judgment for the oppressed: which giveth food to the hungry. The LORD looseth the prisoners: the LORD openeth the eyes of the blind: the LORD raiseth them that are bowed down: the LORD loveth the righteous: the LORD preserveth the strangers; he relieveth the fatherless and widow: but the way of the wicked he turneth upside down. The LORD shall reign for ever, even thy God, O Zion, unto all generations," (Psalm 146:5–10). On this Scripture, Godefridus Udemans, a Dutch preacher, says, "Observe how these words exalt the omnipotence, goodness, truth, righteousness, and mercy of our King. ... Those who do not maintain this truth will not pray according to God's will but according to human fantasy. Therefore, God will not hear them (1 John 5:14)."[28] Paul says, "Continue in prayer, and watch in the same with thanksgiving," (Colossians 4:2). With doxology; it is prescribed in a certain way and manner. David prays, "While I live will I praise the LORD: I will sing praises unto my God while I have any being," (Psalm 146:2). Doxology: a confession and due acknowledgement of the great and manifold excellencies and perfections that are in God. God concurs with your prayers for all things necessary for your salvation, and all your temporal needs. Those who pray as shown in the Lord's Prayer can be certain that God hears them as they pray according to God's will. The Lord "will fulfil the desire of them that fear him: he also will hear their cry, and will save them," (Psalm 145:19). "...thy will be done" (Matthew 26:42). Your obedience must be exact and sincere to the Great King.

In the Lord's Prayer, Christ as King calls for the highest service and worship from you. He is the Great King, and He requires obedience due to Him as King for both His governance and His grace. This means you are to love Him, in prayer and praise, sincerely with an exclusive obedience as the Great King commands, without reservation and that, continually. Such is a universal obedience which answers to His absolute rule as the Hallowed Father in Heaven. And yet, He is a great delight to serve. Is it delightful to you to serve the Great

---

[28] Godefridus Udemans, *The Practice of Faith, Hope, and Love*, (Grand Rapids, MI: Reformation Heritage Books, 2012), 165.

King? He requires that your obedience here on earth is as fit as if it was done in heaven, done before the very throne of the Christ, because all that happens on earth is done before the very throne of the Great King. In His providence and governance, all occurs before His watchful eye. Is there anything that you will persuade Him about, for His kingdom is already of power, and glory, forever, holding forth the keys of death and hell. Do you bring all petitions outlined in this prayer to the King in subjection to His kingship? Every thought, every action, every whisper in the dark, into obedience? Do you *concur* with the rule of the Great King? Do you give universal and sincere obedience, compliance, to the Great King? How, then, do you delight in praising Him for His royal excellency and Kingship? Have you ever thought about that? "I will extol thee, my God, O King," (Psalm 145:1). Does His kingly rule and reign over you employ your tongues in such a way as to shout out His praises for who He is and what He has done with understanding? Consider the prayer then, as it is in full, as we have considered this reigning and ruling of God over our hearts, and take your cue from the Psalms.

Let's end this little book by prayer—it is very Christ-magnifying to pray in this way as the whole prayer now lays out to us:

> I bring glory to you Lord, who in teaching me to call you, Our Father, have taught me not to

confine my love to myself, but to pray also with the affections of a brother to all mankind, and especially of those of the household of faith. I see there are the children of the earth by creation, to all Christians, who are children by adoption for the same heavenly Father. O give me that brotherly kindness to them all, that I may plead the same blessings for them, as for myself, and earnestly pray that they may all share with me in your Fatherly love. In teaching us to pray to Our Father in Heaven, you have taught me the infinite distance between you and us, to pray with the humility of a supplicant with that awe that becomes a frail creature, a miserable sinner, before his Creator, and his Judge. You fill all places, yet your glory is most manifested in heaven, and there your majesty most illustriously dwells, and to your throne there are we to lift up our hearts when we pray. Let my soul fly up to you when I pray in heavenly thoughts and desires, and love. Let me savor nothing of the Earth, whenever I come before you in prayer, as you are in heaven! Let me be heavenly minded. You teach us to seek heaven in the first place. Grant Lord, that I may always plead your blessings in their due order, that I may pray for spiritual blessings with holy violence, with importunity and resolution not to be denied, as being the proper ingredients of your love, and absolutely necessary to my eternal welfare. May your name, your own glorious, and amiable self, be praised by my love and honor of you, being in the Spirit. May your infinite goodness and greatness be forever, by all men and all angels, confessed, and admired, and adored, and magnified both in private and public, in our hearts, our mouths, and our lives. May all creatures share in your goodness, O God. Let all creatures help us to glorify your Name. May every thing that hath breath, praise the Lord. O King of Kings, may your Kingdom of Grace, the church militant, that school of divine love, come to its greatest degree in this life in us. May your Gospel, Lord, be daily propagated, unbelieving nations converted, and the number of your saints increased by the greatness of your Spirit's influence in the world and the church. Grant, O Lord God, that your true religion, your word, your grace, all the holy institutions, laws, and governors, fixed by you in your spiritual Kingdom, may be loved, and honored, and obeyed: and that your faithful subjects may be protected against all the malice of wicked men, or the powers of darkness. Let it be your good pleasure to put an end to sin and misery, to infirmity and death; to complete the number of your elect, and to hasten your Kingdom of glory that we, and all that wait for your salvation, may in the church triumphant eternally love and praise you. Make your Spirit to dominate my life and the life of others around me in your Kingdom. O my God, your will and your commands are most holy, just, and good and condescending to our weakness, and by no means grievous, give me grace to conscientiously observe them, that I may be spiritually persuaded of the truth. Your blessed angels, Lord, always behold your face in heaven, and they have the beatific vision of your perfections and glory to behold, and they cannot but unalterably choose you. They must, of necessity to their utmost capacity praise and love you, they cannot possibly offend you, they forever perfectly obey you, and are always right there to do your bidding and will at your command. And so, the saints too, stick close to you, and your atonement, that whithersoever you go they go. They are completely compliant in everything. Lord, give me grace, in imitation of the blessed spirits above, to set you always before me. Fix my adoration of you to be serious and careful according to your will. Ravish my soul with a lively sense of your infinite perfections. Promise me more glimpses of your goodness in your word. Allow the Spirit-influence of King Jesus to show me how gracious you are, that everything in the world besides you may be tasteless to me. Make my desires always be flying up towards you, that I may render to you, love, and praise, and obedience, pure and cheerful, constant and zealous, universal and uniform, like the holy angels and the saints in heaven render to you always, and do all things according to your will. Lord, I ascribe to you glory, who is the Heavenly Benefactor, who opens your hand, and fills all things living with plenteousness. Let it be your good pleasure to give me, and all who wait on your beneficent love, our food in due season; give us Bread, and all that is comprehended by it, health, food, raiment, and all the necessaries of life. Give us daily bread, nothing to gratify our desire for luxury, but such a competence as your Divine wisdom sees fit for us. Give us, O bountiful Creator, daily bread this day, teach us to live without covetous anxiety for tomorrow, with a trust and dependence on your Fatherly goodness, and to be content and thankful for our present portion, your love has indulged us. Give us Our Bread, that which is our own bread, by honest labor, and grant that we may never eat the bread of idleness, or of deceit. Give us our bread, for unless you give it, we cannot have it, and together with our bread give us your blessing on it, otherwise our bread will not nourish us. Above all, give us the Bread of Life, the Bread that came down from Heaven, the Body and Blood of your most Blessed Son, to feed our souls to eternal life. Blessed Jesus, O that it might be my food, as it was yours, to do the will of your heavenly Father! Lord, for your own infinite mercy's sake, and for the merits of the Son of your love, forgive me, and all penitent sinners our debts, our sins known or secret, of omission or commission, which are the vast debts we owe to your vindictive justice. Forgive us, as we forgive all them, even our greatest enemies that are indebted to us, their debts which are infinitely inconsiderable in comparison of our debts against you. We give you glory, who teaches us love, who has made our forgiveness, the condition of obtaining yours. O gracious condition of pardon, who would not forgive his brother a few pennies in this life, to have ten thousand talents forgiven in the next! O let our love, Lord, learn from your love to us, not only to forgive our enemies, but to be zealous also to do them good, as you do to us. Lord, you see how our enemies, the world, the flesh, and the devil, are every moment soliciting, enticing, alluring, or tempting us to evil. Be merciful to us, save, and help, and deliver us. You see how weak I am, and how ready my own deceitful heart is, to surrender itself to the Tempter; and I know that Satan cannot tempt me without your permission, or mine. Do not lead me, if it is your good pleasure, do not allow me to fall into violent or lasting temptations, that may endanger my perseverance. I know that to be tempted is not sin, for your own beloved Son, God incarnate, was tempted to the most horrid of all sins, to fall down and worship the very devil. I know, Lord, the sin lies in yielding to the temptation. O my God, if you try my love, and lead me into any great temptation, and let me continue under such temptations, your will be done, not mine. But let your tenderness limit and control the Tempter. Let your all-sufficient grace restrain my consent, and keep me always on my guard, watching and praying, and let me at last be more than conqueror in Christ. I am content, Lord, to be tried and assaulted, though it is grievous for those that love you, to be tempted to offend you. O Father of mercy, if you think it fit to lead me into temptation, and yet deliver me from the evil to which I am tempted. Deliver me from the evil of sin, and the evil of punishment, from the evil one, from the evil world, and from my own evil heart, and from all suggestions to evil, for all that is evil is most hateful to you, who are infinite goodness, and most destructive of your love. And therefore, from all that is evil, so defend me; defend your church in the same way. I adore, and love you, Jesus, that the right end of my prayer should be your glory of God, and that I ought to mix praise with my prayers, and to be as zealous to give thanks for what I receive, as to pray for what I desire. On you alone we rely and depend for acceptance, to you alone we offer up our praises, for thine is the Kingdom and Sovereign right to dispose of all things; thine is the power Almighty, to relieve and bless us, thine is the glory. All the communications of your goodness, as they flow from you to your bride, return to you again in sacrifices of love, of praise, and adoration. For the sake of your beloved, in whom all your promises are Amen, and who is Himself the Amen, the faithful and true Witness of your love to us. Hear me, and pardon my wanderings and coldness, and help me to sum up and seal my whole prayer; all my own needs, and all the needs of those I pray for, in a hearty and fervent, and comprehensive, word, in Jesus' name we pray, *AMEN.*

Chapter 10: Conclusion

Ah, dear reader, as we draw the curtain on this humble exposition of the Lord's Prayer—nine sermons woven into a tapestry of divine instruction—let us pause, not in hasty farewell, but in quiet introspection. I confess, as I pen these final words on this crisp September morn in 2025, my own heart stirs with a mix of gratitude and solemnity. For what have we uncovered together but the very heartbeat of communion with God? Not a distant deity, aloof in celestial splendor, but our Father, who beckons us into *His* secret chambers.

Yet, before you set this book aside, perhaps to gather dust on some shelf amid life's clamor, I implore you: turn the mirror inward. Examine your prayers—not with the critic's cold eye, but with the tenderness of a soul seeking truth. How do you pray? What do you pray? And, most piercingly, what does God Himself say about it in His unerring Word?

Picture yourself, as I have so often, kneeling in that private closet Christ prescribed in Matthew 6. The door shut against the world's distractions, the clamor of daily cares silenced for a moment. What words rise from your lips? Are they a torrent of desires, a catalog of needs—health for the body, provision for the wallet, relief from some thorn in the flesh? I remember my own early devotions, fraught with such petitions: "Lord, grant me this success, spare me that trial." Noble enough, perhaps, yet how they echoed the heathens' vain repetitions, supposing volume or eloquence might sway the Immutable One. But oh, the revelation when Scripture's light dawned! God knows your needs before you ask (Matthew 6:8); He is no reluctant benefactor to be *cajoled*. Prayer, as we've seen, is not a lever to move heaven, but a forge *to shape your soul*. Ask yourself: Do my prayers begin with hallowing His name, or do they rush headlong into my own kingdom's demands?

Consider the preface alone—"Our Father which art in heaven." Does this invocation humble you, evoking filial reverence and confidence, as children before a father able and eager to aid? Or do you utter it mechanically, a prelude to your agenda? In my pastoral wanderings, I've encountered souls who pray as isolated beggars, crying "My Father" in selfish silos, forgetting the "Our" that binds us to the covenant family. God says, through Malachi 2:10, "Have we not all one father?" Your prayers, then, must pulse with brotherly affection, interceding for the church's wounds, the lost's salvation.

Reflect: when last did you plead for a brother's deliverance from temptation, or a sister's daily bread, with the fervor you reserve for your *own* trials? If your supplications circle endlessly around self, heed Isaiah's warning: such offerings, devoid of mercy toward others, become an abomination (Isaiah 1:15).

Now, turn to the petitions themselves. "Hallowed be thy name"—ah, how this first cry exposes our prayer's true north! God declares, "Holy and reverend is his name," (Psalm 111:9), yet how often do we profane it with casual chatter? I once prayed with zeal for personal holiness, only to realize my life contradicted my lips—harboring grudges, chasing worldly vanities. What do you hallow in practice? Your prayers must sanctify His titles, attributes, ordinances, Word, and works, setting them apart as holy. If your devotions skim this, leaping to "Give us this day our daily bread," you invert the divine order. God says, through Christ, seek *first* the kingdom (Matthew 6:33); provision follows. Ponder your "daily bread": Is it a humble plea for necessities, trusting His providence, or a veiled demand for luxuries? In seasons of want, I've learned to echo the Psalmist: "The Lord is my shepherd; I shall not want," (Psalm 23:1). Yet, if your prayers fret over tomorrow, ignoring His promise to clothe the lilies, they betray unbelief.

Deeper still, "Thy kingdom come; Thy will be done in earth, as it is in heaven." *What* kingdom do you advance? Is that a strange question? God's Word thunders sovereignty: "The Lord hath prepared his throne in the heavens; and his kingdom ruleth over all," (Psalm 103:19). Your prayers must yearn for *His* reign—Spirit-influenced, fall-reversing—in your heart, your home, the church. But if they cling to earthly empires, resisting submission and government of His power, they war against heaven's pattern. Angels obey with perfect zeal; do you? I've wrestled nights over this, surrendering ambitions that clashed with His decrees. God says, "Not my will, but thine, be done," (Luke 22:42); your prayers must echo Christ's Gethsemane cry, or they remain self-willed rebellion.

Forgiveness follows: "Forgive us our debts, as we forgive our debtors." Here, introspection cuts sharpest. God declares, "If ye forgive not men their trespasses, neither will your Father forgive your trespasses," (Matthew 6:15). Examine your heart: Do grudges fester, debts unforgiven? In my ministry, I've seen people's prayers stalled by bitterness—professions of faith unaccompanied by mercy. What do you pray for absolution while withholding it from others? True prayer confesses sin humbly, extends compassion freely, mirroring the Father's grace.

Then, the plea against evil: "Lead us not into temptation, but deliver us from evil." God tests, but never tempts to sin (James 1:13); yet how do your prayers guard against the world's snares, the flesh's whispers, the devil's schemes? If they ignore self-examination—"Examine yourselves," (2 Corinthians 13:5)—they invite defeat. I've faltered here, yielding to subtle lures, only to find deliverance in watchful supplication. Your prayers must arm you for battle, seeking sanctification amid trials.

Finally, the doxology: "For thine is the kingdom, and the power, and the glory, for ever. Amen." Does praise crown your prayers, ascribing all to Him? God says, "Whoso offereth praise glorifieth me," (Psalm 50:23); yet if your "Amen" seals mere requests, without testimony of His sovereignty, it rings hollow. In my reflections, this has been the capstone: prayer fueling praise, praise igniting prayer.

Beloved, God speaks plainly: Effectual, fervent prayer avails much (James 5:16), but the insensible—ignorant of His will, misaligned with Scripture—profits *naught*. Think on this: Your prayers reveal your soul's posture. Are they sensible, Word-shaped, transformative? Or babbling echoes of self? Repent, if need be; reform your closet. Let this prayer pattern your life, drawing you nearer to the Father. For in sensible prayer, heaven touches earth, and you, dear reader, become a vessel of His glory. To Him—kingdom, power, glory—forever. *Amen.*

Other Works by Dr. McMahon at Puritan Publications

5 Marks of a Biblical Church

5 Marks of a Biblical Disciple

5 Marks of Biblical Commitment to the Visible Body of Christ

5 Marks of Biblical Reformation

5 Marks of Christian Resolve

5 Marks of Devotion to God

A Heart for Reformation

A Primer on the Art of Expository Preaching

A Practical Guide to Primeval History

A Simple Overview of Covenant Theology

A Watchman Over Christ's Church

Augustine's Calvinism: The Doctrines of Grace in Augustine's Writings

Bah Humbug: How Christians Should Think About the Christmas Holiday

Being with Jesus

Christ Commanding His Coronavirus to Covenant Breakers

Christ the Apple Tree and the Joy of True Religion

Covenant Theology Made Easy

Eternity Weighed in the Balance

Following Christ Whithersoever He Goes

Gradual Reformation Intolerable

Historical Theology Made Easy

How Faith Works: Rescuing the Gospel from Contemporary Evangelicalism

How to Live Every Day in the End Times

I Am for You: God's Power in Supporting His People

John 3:16

John Calvin's View of God's Love and the Doctrine of Reprobation

Joseph's Resolve and the Unreasonableness of Sinning Against God

Overcoming Lust In a Sex-crazed World

Practical Observations on the Lord's Prayer

Practical Observations on the Book of Ruth

Practical Observations on the Lord's Supper

Psalm 96: A Theology of Praise 2nd Edition

Reformation of the Heart, Soul and Mind

Save Me: A Study of Psalm 119:89-96

Seeing Christ Clearly

Sophia and the Umbrella – A Children's Book on Justification

Sparks of Divine Glory: A Practical Study of the Attributes of God

Systematic Theology Made Easy

The Cage: A Young Children's Guide to the Biblical Teaching on Hell

The Five Principles of the Gospel

The Kingdom of Heaven is Upon You

The Lord's Voice Cries to the City: A Biblical Guide for Hearing the Word of God Preached

The Reformation Made Easy

The Reformed Apprentice: A Workbook on Reformed Theology (Volumes 1-4)

The Ten Commandments in the Life of the Christian

The Two Wills of God Made Easy

The Two Wills of God: Does God Really Have Two Wills?

The Wickedness, Humiliation, Restoration and Reformation of Manasseh

Umiko and the Mask – Children's Book on Election

Underneath the Blood

Unmasking Self-Flattery in the Church

Walking Victoriously in the Power of the Spirit

www.ingramcontent.com/pod-product-compliance
Lightning Source LLC
LaVergne TN
LVHW091131080826
845145LV00008B/2114
* 9 7 8 1 6 2 6 6 3 5 3 9 5 *